John Heriot

A Historical Sketch of Gibraltar

John Heriot

A Historical Sketch of Gibraltar

ISBN/EAN: 9783337320447

Printed in Europe, USA, Canada, Australia, Japan

Cover: Foto ©Thomas Meinert / pixelio.de

More available books at **www.hansebooks.com**

AN

HISTORICAL SKETCH

OF

GIBRALTAR,

&c. &c.

AN

HISTORICAL SKETCH

OF

GIBRALTAR,

WITH AN

ACCOUNT OF THE SIEGE

WHICH

THAT FORTRESS STOOD

AGAINST THE

COMBINED FORCES OF FRANCE AND SPAIN;

INCLUDING A

MINUTE AND CIRCUMSTANTIAL DETAIL

OF THE

SORTIE

MADE BY THE GARRISON

ON THE MORNING OF NOV. 27, 1781,

FOR THE PURPOSE OF DESTROYING THE FORMIDABLE WORKS
ERECTED BY THE SPANIARDS AGAINST THAT FORTRESS.

LONDON:

PRINTED BY B. MILLAN,
PRINTER TO HIS ROYAL HIGHNESS THE PRINCE OF WALES,
FOR J. EDWARDS, PALL-MALL; T. AND J. EGERTON, WHITE-
HALL; AND W. FADEN, GEOGRAPHER TO THE KING,
STRAND.

1792.

K I N G.

SIRE,

Whilst I humbly offer my most dutiful acknowledgments for the high honour which this Work derives from Your Majesty's gracious condescension, in permitting it to be adorned with the Patronage of Royalty; it becomes me respectfully to express my consciousness, that it is the grandeur of the subject alone which can entitle it to such flattering distinction.

Your

YOUR MAJESTY, from the best information, is already minutely acquainted
with every circumstance of the GLO-
RIOUS DEFENCE made by YOUR GAR-
RISON of GIBRALTAR, during the last
War, against the COMBINED FORCES of
the HOUSE of BOURBON. The gallant
conduct of your Troops upon that occasion, was the admiration of the World:
—but it was BRITONS alone that could
know the powerful incentives which
they had to unparalleled exertion. They
fought under a STANDARD long conse-
crated to *Honour*—and for a PRINCE and a
NATION, to whom they were bound by
every strongest tie of Loyalty, Duty, and
Affection. In *Courage* and in *Sentiment*,
they were as superior to their BESIEG-
ERS, as the *Rock of Gibraltar* towers above
the level of the *Mediterranean Sea*; for,
however much the ARMIES of BOURBON
may have heretofore been distinguished
for Gallantry in the Field, they never felt

that

that *noble and ardent principle*, imbibed under a GOVERNMENT, so singularly combining the Blessings of LIBERTY and LAW, and where the human mind expands under the genial and animating influence of RATIONAL FREEDOM.

The present period seems produced to elucidate the great pre-eminence of the British Constitution, and the exclusive Blessings which BRITONS, under YOUR MAJESTY's mild and just Government, are destined to enjoy. While other Nations are convulsed by the extremes of Anarchy and Licentiousness, this happy Island peculiarly experiences Domestic Peace and National Prosperity, united with the proudest distinctions of Political Grandeur.

To the Wisdom and Vigour of YOUR MAJESTY's Councils are to be imputed, under the Divine Permission, the Blessings

sings which we so fully enjoy, resulting from honourable Peace. From YOUR MAJESTY's Personal Example it is, that your Subjects learn the great Lesson of Human Life---TO BE VIRTUOUS AND HAPPY.

That your Domestic Felicity may continue without alloy, while your Personal Character is considered as the Blessing and Boast of a free and affectionate People, is the dutiful and fervent Prayer of,

SIRE,

YOUR MAJESTY's

Most loyal,

And most devoted

Subject and Servant,

London, May 29th, 1792.   *J. HERIOT.*

ADVERTISEMENT.

THE little Work now offered to the Public, has been thrown together chiefly as an Explanatory Accompaniment to the admirable Print published by Mr. Poggi, descriptive of the *Sortie* made by the GARRISON of GIBRALTAR, on the morning of the 27th of November, 1781, for the purpose of destroying the formidable Works erected by the Spaniards against that Fortress.

To enable those who have patronized, or may possess this great Work, to enter more fully into the nature of the subject, and to form a more enlarged judgment of the Military Glory of the Enterprize, which the Print so minutely and faithfully represents, it was thought expedient to accompany it with something more than a mere detail of the circumstances of the *Sortie*. As short a Sketch as possible is therefore given of the GENERAL HISTORY of GIBRALTAR, and of the LEADING OPERATIONS of the late SIEGE ; in which it has been the study

A   of

of the Writer to be as concise as he could, consistently with the necessary connection and clearness of Historical Narration.

It is with a becoming gratitude that he has to acknowledge his great obligations to the very accurate and interesting Journal of the SIEGE of GIBRALTAR, published by Captain DRINKWATER of the late 72d Regiment, or Royal Manchester Volunteers. The praise of an humble Individual could neither add to his merit as an Historian, nor to his reputation as an Officer. Like the Roman General, though in an inferior military situation, he has not only the glory of having been engaged in, but of faithfully and ably recording the circumstances of, very eminent Military Service. His Book has been received with a degree of avidity and approbation, to which it is richly entitled, as well from the merits of its Author, as from the interesting nature of the subject upon which he writes. Those who wish to peruse the varied occurrences of the glorious defence made by the Garrison of Gibraltar more in detail, the Author of this Work must beg leave to refer to Captain DRINKWATER's History. Those who have already perused it, will not, it is

humbly

humbly hoped, consider as superfluous, the little
Compendium of that History now presented to their
view. It has been endeavoured, by political reflection, to impart something of a new interest to
the Narrative, the propriety and justice of which,
the Author flatters himself, every Briton will sub-
scribe to.

Of the *Sortie*, which, in truth, is the principal
object of this Work, the Author has been enabled,
from the collective information of a number of Officers engaged on that important Service, communicated to him by Mr. Poggi, to give a more minute
and circumstantial detail than has yet been offered
to the World. That single Enterprize forms such
a luminous point in the Military Annals of this
Country, that the Nation must approve with pleasure of every effort that can transmit it, in its brilliant colours, to Posterity. To do this with the most
successful effect, perhaps the Pencil of the Painter
possesses a happier power than the Pen of the Historian. The justice of this remark all will readily
acknowledge, who see the Print executed from a
Drawing by Mr. Poggi, descriptive of that grand
Exploit. This Gentleman, in order to render him-

A 2   self

self perfectly Master of every circumstance relating to this great subject, upon which he wished to occupy his Pencil, soon after the general Pacification took place in 1783, embarked for Gibraltar, where he arrived about the latter end of August of the same year. The gracious reception which he met with from General ELIOTT, convinced him that the recommendations which he had carried with him were of the most flattering and effectual kind. The General gave him a particular invitation to his Table, and did him the honour to say, that from that moment he regarded him as one of his Family. This gratifying mark of distinction was received with suitable acknowledgment, and enjoyed by Mr. POGGI during the ten months of his residence in the Garrison. A few days after his arrival, that illustrious General, with the most flattering condescension, gave him every information relative to the Plan and Execution of the *Sortie*. He further directed his Quarter-Master-General and Aides-de-Camp to give every assistance to Mr. POGGI in the Execution of his intended Work; at the same time shewing him an excellent Plan of the Attack, drawn by Lieutenant KOEHLER of the Corps of Artillery, in which was represented, with the greatest accuracy,

accuracy, the Distribution of the Troops. To all this the General added his permission to Mr. POGGI to visit the Works rebuilt by the Spaniards, upon the same ground and on the same plan with those so successfully demolished by the *Sortie*. No favour or attention, in short, was omitted by General ELIOTT, that could be useful to Mr. POGGI as an Artist, or gratifying to him as a Man.

Than Mr. POGGI, no Artist could be better calculated for the Execution of such a Work. He himself had a Military Education from his Father, who is a native of Corsica, and at this time enjoys a considerable military rank in the service of an Italian Sovereign. From his Education he has derived a degree of Military Enthusiasm, which has enabled him, in some degree, to partake of the Glory of the Subject which his Pencil has treated with so much accuracy, elegance and force, as to transport, in idea, those who were present in the *Sortie*, to the very scene of Action, and to the specific period in which the general Conflagration took place in the Spanish Lines. Such is the testimony which every Officer engaged in that Service, who has seen Mr. POGGI's Drawing, or the Print taken from it, and

now

now given to the World, bears to this great Historical Effort of his Art. It will descend to Posterity, equally a Monument of the Artist's Merit, and of British Glory. Should this little Work be deemed worthy to accompany it, the Author will have reason to esteem himself fortunate in having formed an alliance with an Art, better calculated to establish a higher and more lasting celebrity, than the feeble effort of his Pen.

Mr. Poggi, in the Execution of this Work, has not been without that Patronage which is best calculated to encourage Genius, and stimulate Exertion. His MAJESTY, with that gracious condescension and refined taste which have led the Arts to fix their residence in Britain, honoured Mr. Poggi's Drawing, as soon as it was finished, with his particular attention, and spontaneous Patronage.— Under the animating Eye of Royalty has this Work been finished, after *eight years labour*, and at the particular suggestion of His MAJESTY it was, that Three Additional Plates were added to the Print, to render the Scene as complete as it was represented in the Original Drawing. This Print, thus completed, Mr. Poggi has been honoured with the

gracious

gracious Permission of His MAJESTY to lay at his feet; an act of condescension in the Sovereign which the Artist most gratefully feels, and which, from the peculiar nature of the subject, the BRITISH ARMY will receive as a tribute of particular regard to their brilliant exertions, and an additional incitement to future emulative enterprize. It must impart likewise new vigour to the Arts, for it confirms the flattering decision, THAT NEXT TO THE GLORY of HAVING ACTED NOBLY, IS THE MERIT of ABLY RECORDING THAT ACTION.

HISTORICAL SKETCH

OF

GIBRALTAR, &c.

- ━━━

IT has been a received axiom amongst men, that with the Progress of Civilization and Science, the Spirit for Military Enterprize becomes proportionably on the decline. The Love of Gain, instilled by the pursuits of Commerce, it has been established as an opinion, imperceptibly undermines the Love of Glory; and as Commerce flourishes best in the tranquil security of Peace, for the benefits which it yields, men have become willing to sacrifice the splendor and sublimity of Military Achievement.

To Britons, however, it must be matter of honest congratulation, that, while in Commercial Enterprize they rank as the First Nation of the World, they still likewise are the First in Military Fame. The warlike Genius of Britain, which blazed at Azincourt, and thundered on the Plains of Cressy; which reaped the Laurels of Blenheim, and rushed to Victory at Minden, may slumber in the calm of Peace; but when occasion calls, can rouse itself with re-animated vigour.

The Military Spirit of this Country never soared a more glorious flight, than during the critical and eventful period of the last War. Our Navy rode triumphant in the Wes-

B   tern

tern Hemisphere, where several brilliant and important
Victories were obtained; and in the East, in many hard
fought Actions, it baffled the superior power of France.
In America, the invincible bravery of the British Army,
on all occasions, was sufficient to avert the disgrace attendant upon the general misconduct of the War; while in
the East, our Forces never met the Enemy in the field but
to gain the most decisive Victories.

At Gibraltar, however, it was, that the brightest Laurels
were to be won. The eyes of Europe were turned to that
little spot, with hope or apprehension, as different political
interests suggested; and the fate of Britain was considered
in a great measure to hang upon the success of the formidable Force which was collected against it.

The Defence made by that Garrison must ever shine with
distinguished character in the Annals of Military Glory;
and will irradiate, to future times, the auspicious Reign
of GEORGE the THIRD, with no secondary lustre. While
all the virtues and blessings of Peace decorate and surround
his Throne, his Arms have achieved in every quarter of
the Globe the brightest Military Trophies; and the future Historian, when he comes to record, and to dwell with
rapture on the circumstances of (what every good Subject
will ardently pray for) a long, very long and happy Reign,
he will find it difficult to suit his Eulogium to the Domestic
Blessings which have flowed from so excellent a Prince, or
to the variety of Military Splendor which has, at different
periods, marked the Operations of his Arms.

The very name of Gibraltar revives in the bosom of
every Briton the spark of Military Ardour. It is justly
considered

considered as the brightest Jewel of the British Crown; which no Boon, however splendid and valuable, could induce the Nation ingloriously to barter. The possession of this Fortress yields indeed to Great Britain, not only signal Political, but great Commercial Advantages. It is reckoned by Europe the Key to the Mediterranean Ocean, and consequently of singular benefit in carrying on the Trade of the Levant. In its remaining subject to the British Empire, therefore, not only the British Nation, but every Northern Maritime Power of Europe, is greatly interested; for under the Batteries of the Garrison the vessels of all Nations find at all times a safe and ready asylum, either in their ingress to, or egress from the Mediterranean Sea.

Were this Fortress subject to Spain, there can be no doubt but the case would be very different. The imposition of heavy duties at the Port of Gibraltar would have a fatally restrictive operation upon the Trade of the Mediterranean; and every Maritime Nation would be, with respect to that Trade, at all times in the power of Spain. To the possession of Gibraltar there are therefore attached great Commercial Benefits, as well as Military Splendor; the united considerations of which must at all times stimulate the Nation to preserve it as one of the most valuable appendages to the British Empire.

GIBRALTAR is a part of Andalusia, the most southern province of Spain, to which it is connected by a low isthmus of sand. The Rock is seven miles in circumference, forming a promontory three miles in length, and presenting the most singular natural appearance. It has indeed been distinguished in the earliest Annals of European Nations. The Historians of Rome have recorded Gibraltar as of

B 2   celebrity,

celebrity, under the title of *Mons Calpé*, and distinguished it, and *Mons Abyla*, on the opposite Coast of *Africa*, by the mythological appellation of *the Pillars of Hercules*. This Rock, however, cast in the mould of Nature as an impregnable Fortress, it does not appear that any of the Antients inhabited. Their knowledge and practice of the Military Art were not indeed suited to improve the natural advantages of such a place. These seem to have been disregarded till the beginning of the Eighth Century, when the Saracens from Africa invaded Spain, and subjugated the Country.

The Saracen Leader to whom the Expedition against Spain was committed, was named TARIF, and in order to secure a communication with Africa, he thought of erecting a Castle on *Mons Calpé*, on the isthmus at the foot of which he had landed his Forces. The remains of this Castle, which was erected about the year 725, are still to be seen in the Garrison of Gibraltar.

In compliment to TARIF, the name of the Rock was changed by the Saracens from *Mons Calpé* to *Gibel Tarif*, signifying the *Mountain* of *Tarif*, and thence by an easy corruption, it came to be denominated *Gibraltar*.

TARIF having driven the Goths, who had inhabited Spain for a period of upwards of three hundred years, into the Northern Provinces of the Empire, made himself master of all those to the South. The Saracens, from the luxuriancy of the Country, and the natural operation of the Climate, soon declined into habits of indolence and effeminacy; while the exiled Goths retrieved, in the provinces of Biscay, Asturias, &c. in which they had found

an

an asylum, their Military Ardour, and began in their turn to make successful reprisals upon their Arabic Conquerors.

Gibraltar, during these transactions, had gained some little importance as a place of strength ; but Algeziras, a City founded on the opposite side of the Bay, and to which the Saracens paid a more particular attention, was now become a Fortress of great magnificence and note. This celebrated City seems, indeed, to have almost wholly obscured Gibraltar in the Histories of those times, for very little mention is made of the latter till the beginning of the Fourteenth Century, when FERDINAND, King of Castile, with a small force, took it from the Infidels.

Gibraltar remained in the hands of the Spaniards till the year 1333, when ABOMELIQUE, son of the Emperor of Fez, landing at Algeziras, to the succour of the Moorish King of Grenada, laid siege to Gibraltar, and in five months starved the Garrison into a Surrender. An unsuccessful attempt was made by ALONZO XI. then on the Throne of Castile, to recover the Fortress, a few days after its Surrender to the Moors. In 1343, ALONZO took Algeziras, after a most memorable Siege. Impatient under his former disgrace, he resolved again to attempt the Recovery of Gibraltar, and in 1349, profiting by Intestine Commotions in Africa, he sat down before it with a very formidable Force.

The Moors, after the loss of Algeziras, paid great attention to fortifying Gibraltar, and they had now rendered it a place of very considerable strength. Their Garrison was also numerous, and well provided, and consisted of

their

their choicest troops. In the beginning of 1350, when
ALONZO had almost reduced the besieged to a Capitula-
tion, a pestilential disorder broke out in his Camp, which,
amongst numbers of his soldiers, carried off himself; upon
which the Spaniards immediately raised the Siege.

In 1410, JUSAF III. King of Grenada, got possession
of the Rock; but the Inhabitants, averse to the Government of their new Masters, revolted against the Grenadian
Alcaide, and again threw themselves under the protection
of the Emperor of Morocco, who dispatched his Brother
SAYD, with 3000 troops, to their assistance.

The King of Grenada, on the following year, appeared
before the place with a Fleet and Army; and having worst-
ed SAYD in several skirmishes, forced him to retreat within the Castle, where being closely besieged, and reduced
to great extremity for want of provisions, he was at last
obliged to submit.

In 1642, it was dismembered from the Empire of Grenada by the Duke de MEDINA SIDONIA, and added to
the Crown of Castile and Leon, under HENRY IV. The
Duke, with very little interruption, enjoyed the possession
of it till the Reign of FERDINAND and ISABELLA in 1502,
when it was finally annexed to the Crown of Spain.

In the Reign of CHARLES V. the fortifications of the
town were modernized, and considerably extended and increased, after which it was thought to be impregnable.

It remained in the quiet possession of the Crown of
Spain from this period till the year 1704, when it was unexpectedly

expectedly wrested from that Power, it is to be hoped for ever, by an English Squadron, under the command of Sir GEORGE ROOKE.

This Admiral had been sent into the Mediterranean with a strong Fleet, in the Spring of 1704, to assist CHARLES, Archduke of Austria, in obtaining the Crown of Spain; but his Instructions being limited, there was nothing of importance that he could effect. Unwilling to return to England, with a powerful Squadron, without having at-chieved something, he called a Council of War on the 17th of July, 1704, near Tetuan, to whom he proposed seve-ral schemes of Attack; particularly a second attempt upon Cadiz, which, however, was judged impracticable from the want of a sufficient number of Land Forces. After much deliberation, it was resolved to make a sudden and vigorous Attack upon Gibraltar.

On the 21st of the same month the Fleet reached the Bay, and 1800 men, English and Dutch, commanded by the Prince of HESSE D'ARMSTADT, were immediately landed on the Isthmus. The Garrison was then summoned in form, but the Governor refusing to surrender, preparations were made for the Attack. By day-break on the 23d, the ships appointed to cannonade the town, under Admirals BYNG and VANDERDUSSEN, with those destined to batter the New Mole, commanded by Captain HICKS, were at their several stations. The signal was immediately made by the Admiral for the commencement of the Cannonade, which was executed with such spirit and effect, that the Enemy, in five or six hours, were driven from their guns, almost in every quarter, but most completely from the New Mole Head. Captain WHITAKER, with the armed

boats,

boats, was ordered to possess himself of that post ; but Captains HICKS and JUMPER, who lay with their ships nearest the Mole, eager to share in every part of the glory, pushed ashore in their barges, before the other boats could come up. Upon their landing, the Spaniards sprung a mine upon them, which blew up the Fortifications, killed two Lieutenants and forty men, and wounded sixty. The Assailants, however, kept possession of the work, and being joined by Captain WHITAKER, boldly advanced, and took a small bastion, half-way betwixt the Mole and the Town. The Marquis de SALINES, who was Governor, being again summoned, thought proper to surrender. Hostages were exchanged, and on the following day, the 24th, the Prince of HESSE took possession of the Gates.

The works were very strong, mounting one hundred pieces of ordnance, well appointed with ammunition and stores ; but the Garrison consisted only of one hundred and fifty regular troops. These marched out with the Honours of War, and such of the Spaniards as chose to remain, were allowed the same privileges that they had formerly enjoyed in a similar situation. The loss of the English in this Attack, was two Lieutenants, one Master, fifty-seven Sailors, killed : one Captain, seven Lieutenants, one Boatswain, two hundred and seven Sailors wounded.

Though the Spanish Garrison was so small, yet when the natural strength of the place is considered, with the very respectable state in which the Fortifications even then were, the Capture of Gibraltar must be allowed to be a very brilliant achievement. Perhaps the invincible impetuosity natural to British Sailors, was better calculated for

such

such an enterprize, than the systematic operation of a regular Force. In War, that is often gained by a sudden and
vigorous effort, which much greater numbers shall deli-
berately attempt in vain. It has since been sufficiently
proved, how little impression a very superior Army, using
every means of assault which the Art of War can supply,
has been able to effect: With a British Garrison, Gibraltar may be considered as impregnable. It is only by
Famine that it ever can be endangered ; but while Britain
remains the Mistress of the Ocean, it is to be hoped that
risk can barely be admitted to exist.

After the British Colours were first displayed upon the
Rock of Gibraltar, the Prince of HESSE remained Governor of the place, and as many men as could be spared from
the Fleet, were left as a Garrison.

The Courts of Madrid and Paris were greatly concerned
at the loss of this important Fortress, and every means
were concerted for a vigorous attempt for its recovery.
The Prince made every disposition for a resolute Defence,
and being informed that the Army of the Besiegers was to
be assisted by a Naval Force from Toulon, he sent advice
to Sir JOHN LEAKE, who had been left at Lisbon by Sir
GEORGE ROOKE, on his return to England, with a squadron
of eighteen ships of war, for the purpose of giving succour
to the Garrison of Gibraltar. Sir JOHN prepared for his
duty ; but in the mean time a Fleet of French ships arrived in the Bay of Gibraltar, and landed six Battalions,
which joined the Spanish Army. The French Squadron
thereafter proceeded to the westward, leaving only six
frigates in the Bay.

C   On

On the 11th of October, the Marquis de VILLADA-
RIAS, a Grandee of Spain, who commanded the Army of
the Allies, opened his trenches against the Town; soon
after which Sir JOHN LEAKE arrived with twenty sail of
English and Dutch men of war: learning, however, that
the Enemy were coming upon him with a superior Force,
he thought it most eligible to return to the Tagus, and equip
his Fleet, that he might be in a better condition to supply
and assist the Garrison in a second Expedition, for which
he had prudently directed preparations to be made at Lisbon
during his present cruize. On the 25th he was again
enabled to sail from the Tagus, completely equipped, and
on the 29th unexpectedly entering the Bay of Gibraltar, he
surprized three frigates and a fire ship of the Enemy, with
some prizes and other vessels.

He then landed the reinforcements, and supplied the
Garrison with six months provisions and ammunition, at
the same time detaching on shore a body of five hundred
Sailors to assist in repairing the breaches made in the Works
by the Enemy's fire. The arrival of the Admiral was
critical and opportune; for on that very night the Marquis
had resolved on an Attack by sea and land, at five different
points, for which purpose two hundred boats had been
collected.

Thus completely defeated in their present designs, the
Spaniards still entertained hopes of taking the Fortress;
and supposing that the Garrison would be less vigilant
whilst the Fleet was in the Bay, they formed the extravagant and desperate scheme of surprising them, though the
British Admiral was before the Town. On the 31st
of October, five hundred Volunteers took the Sacra-
ment,

ment, never to return till they had planted the Spanish Flag on the Battlements of Gibraltar. This forlorn Party was conducted by a goat-herd to the south side of the Rock, near the Cave Guard, (at that time called the Pass of Locust Trees.) They mounted the Rock, and during the first night lodged themselves unperceived in St. Michael's Cave. On the succeeding night they scaled CHARLES the Fifth's Wall, and surprized and massacred the Guard at Middle Hill. By the assistance of ropes and ladders they got up several hundreds of the party appointed to sustain them ; but being, during this operation, discovered, a strong detachment of Grenadiers marched up from the Town, and attacked them with such spirit, that one hundred and sixty of them were killed or forced over the precipice, and a Colonel and thirty Officers, with the remainder, taken Prisoners. These brave but unfortunate Adventurers, were to have been supported by a body of French Troops, and different feints were to have been made below, to distract the attention of the Garrison ; but from some disagreement amongst the Commanding Officers on the Plan of Attack, they were basely abandoned to their fortune.

Sir JOHN LEAKE, mean while, did not lie inactively before the Town, but whilst he remained in the Bay, was continually alarming the Enemy on their coasts. On the 22d of November he had information, by one of his Cruizers, that a strong Squadron was fitting out at Cadiz, which would soon be ready for sea; and receiving further intelligence, that a Convoy had sailed from Lisbon for the relief of the Garrison, he prepared to join them off Lagos, in order to conduct them in safety, but was confined within the Straits by a westerly wind.

The

The Prince, mean while, was vigilant in frustrating the Enemy's designs, who flattered themselves, that on the arrival of their Fleet from Cadiz, Sir JOHN would be obliged to retire, and the Garrison to surrender to their united attack. · Their fire upon the Rock was continued with increased vivacity, in consequence of which many guns were dismounted, and the Works materially injured in different parts.

On the 7th of September, part of the long wished for succours arrived, and on the two following days the remainder came in, consisting in all, of near two thousand men, with proportionable ammunition and provisions, after having made a narrow escape from the Enemy's Fleet off Cape Spartel. It was now no longer thought essential to detain the Fleet in the Bay, or on the coast, especially as Mons. POINTIS was expected with a very superior force.

The Spanish General having at this period been likewise reinforced with a very considerable body of Infantry, made, on the 11th of January, 1705, a very spirited attack, with only sixty Grenadiers, on the Works at the extremity of the King's Lines; but two Officers, and several of the Soldiers being killed, the remainder of the Party retreated. This was probably only meant as an experiment of the vigilance and alacrity of the Garrison ; for not discouraged by the repulse, the attack was repeated, early on the succeeding day, by five or six hundred Grenadiers, French and Walloons, supported by one thousand Spaniards, under Lieutenant General TUY. Their object was to storm a breach which had been made in the Round Tower at the extremity of the King's Lines, and another in the intrenchment on the Hill. The retrenchment which

covered

covered the latter breach, with part of the intrenchment joining the precipice of the Rock, was guarded at night by a Captain, three Subalterns, and ninety men; but it was customary for the Captain to withdraw at day-break, with two Subalterns and sixty of his Guard. The Round Tower was occupied by one hundred and eighty men, under the command of a Lieutenant Colonel.

The Spanish Commandant, by Deserters from the Garrison, had obtained circumstantial intelligence of the strength of those posts, and concerted his attack accordingly. The Assaulting Party for the upper breach mounted the Rock at dead of night, and concealed themselves in its clefts till the Captain, with his detachment, had withdrawn. They then climbed to the point of the intrenchment, and throwing grenades on the Subaltern and his little party, obliged them to retreat. At the same instant three hundred of the Assailants stormed the Round Tower, where Lieutenant Colonel BARR made a vigorous defence, though the Enemy having passed the breach above, annoyed him on the flank with great stones and grenades. Observing, however, the Spaniards moving down to cut off his communication with the Town, he retired, and by getting over the parapet of the King's Lines, descended into the covert way, where the English Guards were posted. By this time the whole Garrison was alarmed, and all the Regiments were at their stations. Captain FISHER gallantly endeavoured to stop the progress of the Enemy with only seventeen men, but was repulsed, and himself taken Prisoner. At length Lieutenant Colonel MONCAL, with four or five hundred men, charged the Assailants with such bravery, that they were repulsed in their turn, and the Tower was retaken, after it had been in
their

their possession for more than an hour. Soon after this attack, the Garrison was reinforced by six Companies of Dutch troops and two hundred English Soldiers, with provisions and stores.

The Allies of Bourbon were still bent upon the recovery of Gibraltar. The pride of Spain was deeply wounded by its remaining a Garrison of England, and with that Court, to retrieve the disgrace attendant on its loss was the first object of the War. The Marquis de VILLADARIAS was superseded by the Marshal TASSE, a French Officer of reputation in the Art of War; and Monsieur POINTIS, with a strong squadron under his command, was directed to co-operate with the Marshal, by blocking up the Port. The Marshal carried with him to Camp four fresh Batta-. lions, besides other succours. The Ordnance which had been injured by use, was entirely changed, and the Works were put in the best state of repair.

In Britain, these preparations were not disregarded. The English Minister, fully sensible of the importance of Gibraltar, ordered a Squadron under Sir THOMAS DILKES, and Sir JOHN HARDY, to join that under the command of Sir JOHN LEAKE, at Lisbon. The junction being effected, and his own Fleet refitted, Sir JOHN, on the 6th of March, left the Tagus with twenty-eight English, four Dutch, and eight Portuguese men of war, having on board two Battalions. Fortunately for the besieged, the incessant rains about this period had retarded the Marshal's operations, and greatly incommoded M. POINTIS, eight of whose ships were forced from their anchors by the strong westerly wind, and obliged on the 9th to drive up the Mediterranean. Such was their situation when

the

the British Admiral entered the Straits; and about half past five, on the morning of the 10th, was almost abreast of Cabrita Point. The remaining part of the French Squadron put to sea on his approach, and Sir JOHN discovering five sail making out of the Bay, and a gun fired at them from the Garrison, concluded that the Town was safe, and immediately gave chace. The English Fleet soon brought the French ships to Action, in which three of the line were taken, and the Admiral's ship and another forced on shore and burnt. Sir JOHN afterwards looked into Malaga, where the ships that had been driven from the Bay, had taken shelter: but, hearing the report of the guns, they had fled to Toulon. Sir JOHN, giving up the pursuit, returned to Gibraltar, which was now so well supplied, that Marshal TASSE withdrew his troops from the trenches, and formed a Blockade, drawing an intrenchment across the Isthmus, to prevent the Garrison from ravaging the country.

In the course of this Siege, the Besiegers did not lose fewer than 10,000 men, including those who died of sickness, &c. The Garrison lost about four hundred.

The Prince of HESSE, who had derived so much honour from its successful Defence against the combined Forces of the Allies, remained in the place while the Batteries were repairing; he at the same time made some judicious improvements in the Fortifications, and left the Garrison much stronger than it was before the commencement of the Siege. The Prince then joined the Arch-Duke CHARLES at Lisbon, where the combined Fleets of England and Holland were assembled, to support that Prince in his pretensions to the Crown of Spain.

As

As the Arch-Duke was resolved to try his fortune with the Earl of PETERBOROUGH, in Valencia and Catalonia, the Prince of HESSE was sent back to Gibraltar, to prepare part of the Garrison to embark, and soon after was followed by the Fleet, having on board the Arch-Duke, who was received by the Garrison as lawful Sovereign of Spain.

On the 5th of August they proceeded for Valencia, having taken on board the English Guards, and three old Regiments, two new Battalions only being left behind as a Garrison, as no danger was to be apprehended from the Enemy in that quarter.

Major General RAMOS, who had served there during the Siege, was appointed Governor of Gibraltar by the King, and took possession of his Government with a reinforcement of four hundred men. He soon afterwards resigned, and was succeeded by Colonel ROGER ELLIOT, during whose Government, in April 1706, Gibraltar was made a Free Port, by a Special Order of Her Majesty, QUEEN ANNE.

The pride of the Spaniards was deeply wounded by Gibraltar still remaining subject to the British Crown. They regarded it with a watchful and envious eye, and the whole Policy of their Court seems to have had for its aim, at that period as well as during every succeeding one, the recovery of this Fortress. Accordingly, in 1720, it was threatened by them again.

Ceuta, a Spanish Fortress in Barbary, had then been besieged many years by the Moors, and a formidable Force, commanded by the Marquis de LEDA, was assembled

assembled in Gibraltar Bay, under pretence of relieving it, but with a secret intention of first surprizing Gibraltar ; for which purpose scaling-ladders, and every necessary implement for an Assault, were provided. The British Minister, apprised of their Armament, and suspecting some *finesse*, dispatched orders to Colonel KANE, Governor of Minorca, immediately to embark a part of his Garrison, and repair to Gibraltar, under convoy of the Fleet then in the Mediterranean. On his arrival, he found that Fortress in a very critical situation, the Garrison consisting only of three weak Battalions, commanded by Major HETHERINGTON, who, except Major BATTEROUX, was the only Field Officer in the place. Many Officers were absent; there were only fourteen days provisions in the Stores; many Spaniards in the Town, and a Fleet before its walls. Such was the critical posture of affairs when this Reinforcement of five hundred men arrived, with Provisions and Ammunition. The British Commodore afterwards acted with so much spirit, that the Marquis de LEDA was obliged to sail for Ceuta, though he continued of opinion that the Garrison might have been taken by a General Assault.

This crafty design of the Spanish Court being thus defeated, Gibraltar remained unmolested till the year 1726, when an Army was assembled in the neighbourhood of Algeziras. On the 20th of January following, they encamped on the plain below St. Roque, and began to erect a Battery on the beach, to protect their Camp. Though Admiral HOPSON was then at anchor in the Bay with a very formidable fleet, yet as he had no intelligence of the commencement of Hostilities between Great Britain and Spain, he was reluctantly compelled to overlook the

D   trans-

transporting Provisions, Artillery, and Ammunition, to the Camp from Algeziras, where the Spaniards had formed their magazines. Brigadier KANE, who had been a second time ordered from Minorca to Gibraltar, lay under a similar embarrassment with the Admiral. The operations of the Spaniards, however, tending to a direct Attack upon the Garrison, he thought it prudent to dismiss all of that Nation from the Town, and to forbid their gallies from anchoring under his guns.

Since any preceding attempt of the Spaniards upon this Fortress, it had undergone considerable alterations, and been very materially improved ; several Works had been erected on the heights above the Lines, called *Willis's* Batteries ; the Prince's Lines were extended to the extremity of the Rock, and an inundation was formed out of the morass in front of the Grand Battery, which gave it very great additional security.

The Spanish Army consisted of near 20,000 men, commanded by the Count de las TORRES, who, soon after his Camp was formed, advanced within reach of the Garrison. The Brigadier therefore dispatched a Parley, to desire, " That he would withdraw from the range of his " guns, otherwise he should do his utmost to force " him." The COUNT haughtily replied, " That, as " the Garrison could command no more than they had " the power to maintain, he should obey His CATHOLIC " MAJESTY's Orders, and encroach as far as he was " able." The Brigadier, notwithstanding, still waved hostility, till the Spaniards, by their proceedings, should provoke him to it, in the absolute defence of his command.

In

In the beginning of February, a considerable reinforcement reached the Garrison, under the command of Brigadier CLAYTON, the Lieutenant-Governor, who now assumed the command. This was conveyed on board Sir CHARLES WAGER's Fleet. Soon after, the Spaniards encroaching upon the neutral ground, for the purpose of erecting works against the Garrison, this was considered as an act of open hostility, and on the 11th of February, the Lieutenant-Governor opened his Batteries upon them. They persisted nevertheless in carrying on the work, and began to construct a mine under *Willis's*, with an intention, if possible, to blow up that Battery. By the close of the month, and early in the following, the Enemy were enabled to open three Batteries, mounting fifty-four guns, besides mortars. The Besieged were not inactive, but on their part kept up a constant and well-directed fire from all the Batteries that bore upon the Enemy's Works. The Fleet, mean while, did every thing in their power to distress the Enemy; but on the 12th of April, after several reinforcements had been thrown into the Garrison, both from England and Minorca, the Admirals sailed with the main body of the Fleet to the westward, leaving Commodore DAVIES in the Bay with six ships of the line and several small vessels.

The Lieutenant-Governor made several attempts to dislodge the Enemy from the Cave under *Willis's*, but without effect.

On the 21st of the same month, Lord PORTMORE, the Governor, arrived with a Battalion of the Guards, and another of the Line, accompanied by several of the Nobility, who went to serve as Volunteers. On the

D 2   26th,

26th, the COUNT opened a new Battery against *Willis's*, and the extremity of the Prince's Lines. Their Batteries now mounted sixty cannon, besides mortars. In the beginning of May, the Garrison had intelligence that the Enemy intended an Assault, and every necessary precaution was consequently taken by the former, for a vigorous defence. In the mean time, the Spaniards continued to extend and improve their Works, and the Garrison were receiving seasonable supplies of Ammunition. The firing continued on both sides till the 12th of June, when about ten at night, Col. FITZGERALD, of the Irish Brigade, beat a Parley, and being admitted into the Garrison, delivered letters to Lord PORTMORE from the Dutch Minister at the Court of Madrid, with a copy of the Preliminaries of a General Peace; in consequence of which, a mutual suspension of hostilities immediately took place.

In 1729, the Parliament of Great Britain addressed His Majesty KING GEORGE II. to take especial care, in the Treaty then pending, to preserve Gibraltar and the Island of Minorca under the dominion of the British Crown. The Nation were now fully sensible of the vast importance of both these places, but more particularly of the former; and the Parliament took the alarm at overtures having been made to restore it, for a valuable consideration, to the Crown of Spain. The Ministers of that time, finding it a measure highly unpopular, wisely relinquished the idea, and Gibraltar has ever since continued, and it is to be hoped, ever will continue, to be the most honourable appendage to the British Crown.

The succeeding period of the History of Gibraltar has tended considerably to increase its importance to this country,

country, which indeed is now so generally acknowledged, that any future Minister, who, from whatever motive, or for whatever consideration, should form the plan of transferring it to any Foreign Sovereignty, would probably forfeit more than either his popularity or his place.

The recovery of Gibraltar has been the leading object in every War into which Spain has entered, during the present Century, against this Kingdom, and it has invariably been the point to which their principal operations have diverged. It was the policy of the old Court of France insidiously to cherish the eager desire of Spain for the recovery of that Fortress, for it at all times rendered that Ally subservient to the deep intrigue of the Gallic Cabinet. The hope, however extravagant, of repossessing Gibraltar, was at all times sufficient to stimulate Spain to a ready confederation in hostility, nor had repeated experience proved to her, that her utmost efforts were in vain. The resources of Spain have been often drained in unavailing Sieges, and that force has idly spent its rage against the Rock, which might otherwise have been successfully employed in the dismemberment of the British Empire.

The most convincing and glorious proof of the importance of this Fortress, remains yet to be narrated; and it is happily of a date so recent, as to adorn the æra in which we live.

From the close of the Siege in 1727, little that is very material presents itself in the History of Gibraltar, till the commencement of the last War with the House of Bourbon. In the year 1760, during the Government of the Earl of HOME, an incident occurred, which, however, is

doubtless

doubtless worthy of record. Two British Regiments had been a very considerable time on that station, and from the continuance of the War at that period, saw little prospect of being relieved. A conspiracy was formed by the discontented Soldiers, to surprize, plunder, and massacre their Officers, and after seizing the Military Chest, to purchase for themselves a secure retreat, by delivering the Fortress into the hands of the Spaniards. The Conspirators amounted to no fewer than seven hundred and thirty. Their number, though it promised them more certain success in the execution of their plot, yet subjected them to a greater risk of previous discovery. An accidental quarrel in a Wine House led to a detection, and the Ringleaders were punished with a vigorous, but necessary and just severity.

During the long War which succeeded the year 1757, and which proved, under the Administration of a PITT, so glorious to the British Arms, it does not appear that the Spaniards were in a condition to attempt the Siege of Gibraltar. The British Fleet rode so triumphant in every quarter of the Globe, that we were enabled to assail our Enemies in their most valuable possessions, and the success of our Enterprizes in the Western Hemisphere against the richest Colonies of Spain, together with the capture of several of her ships, freighted with her annual supply of treasure, not only disabled her from any great attempt, but sunk that Nation in despondence and despair. Gibraltar therefore, during the whole of that War, enjoyed a state of uninterrupted tranquillity.

During the absence of the Hon. General CORNWALLIS, who had been appointed Governor, Major General BOYD, the Lieutenant-Governor, enjoyed the command; and

under

under his government the Garrison was considerably strengthened by three new bastions on the sea line, and additional improvements at the Southward.

The disturbances in the British Colonies in America, revived the hopes of the Spanish Court, which still brooded with a sullen enmity over the loss of Gibraltar, and the repeated subsequent disgraces which it had experienced before that Fortress. It saw France with pleasure insidiously fanning the flame of Rebellion which was ready to burst out in the British North American Colonies, and with alacrity entered into all the views of the French Court against the British Empire. The Spaniards flattered themselves with the hope, that Great Britain would be so overwhelmed by the variety of difficulties which she would have to encounter, from an extended and arduous warfare on the continent of America, and from the combined hostilities of the House of Bourbon in Europe, that she would find it impossible to sustain Gibraltar against the powerful force which they meditated to send against it. Such was the reasoning of the Cabinet of Spain so early as the year 1774. At this period, it seemed the wish of every European Power to concur in a general plan for crushing the British Empire. By the intrigues of the French Court at that of St. Petersburgh, and some others in the North of Europe, the *Armed Neutrality* was projected, and readily acceded to; a formidable combination, which though not *actively* so, was secretly *hostile* to Great Britain. At the head of this Armed Neutrality was placed the EMPRESS of RUSSIA, whose Navy had been nursed by the unsuspecting generosity of Britain, and reared by her into respect.

Expe·

Experience had taught the Court of Spain, that some new and more impressive mode of Attack must be devised for the reduction of Gibraltar, than any they had practised before. The example of 1705, and afterwards of 1727, during which Siege they had for three years, with fruitless toil, raised expensive Works against the land side, convinced them that additional means must be employed, and Spanish Generals of reputation, unanimously concurred in the necessity of a co-operating Attack by sea. In the year 1774, therefore, an order was issued throughout all the Colleges, or Military Seminaries of the Kingdom of Spain, that they should suspend all Studies but those which had for their object the Mode of Attack upon Fortified Places by Sea and Land.

At this period it was, that His CATHOLIC MAJESTY confided his scheme for the Reduction of Gibraltar, to his favourite, the DUKE de CRILLON, who had presided at a Military Court appointed by the King in 1770, to examine and discuss every project that could be adopted into the system of Attack by Sea ; a system pronounced to be practicable against Gibraltar, since the conclusion of the preceding War, when M. de VALLIERE, an able French Engineer, was called into Spain in the year 1762.

These preparatory proceedings of the Spanish Cabinet, were not so secretly transacted, but they were intimated to the Court of London early in the year 1776, and the ultimate object of them with sufficient precision ascertained. Amidst the important considerations which the commencement of the American War demanded of the British Ministry, the formidable Attack meditated against Gibraltar

was

was not overlooked. His MAJESTY justly conceived, that upon the proper choice of a Commandant for that Fortress, much of its future safety would depend, and in the same year, of his own free will, named General ELIOTT to that Government, who took possession of it early in the following year. The judicious election of the Sovereign, a series of important event was speedily to confirm; and though it were unjust to suppose, that many General Officers in the service of Great Britain would not, in the same situation, have acquitted themselves with honour, yet the mind of General ELIOTT seemed peculiarly formed for the arduous and hazardous service in which he was to be engaged.

Under the command of Lieutenant General BOYD, it has been observed, the Fortifications of Gibraltar were considerably strengthened. General ELIOTT continued to make such additions as seemed further necessary, but the amicable communication between the Garrison and the neighbouring Inhabitants of Spain, continued to subsist, till the 21st of June, 1779, when it was closed by a special order from the Court of Madrid. That Court, having matured its preparations, thought it no longer necessary to wear the mask of hypocrisy; but as no reasonable pretext immediately offered for a Declaration of War against Great Britain, it was resolved to make one. A sham Mediation was interposed, and such terms offered to Great Britain, as it was impossible for her, without hesitation, not to reject. This was what the Spanish Court aimed at, and they now entered with alacrity into the War.

Before any reply, however, was given by the British Ministry to the Pacific Propositions of the Spanish Cabinet,

E   over-

overtures had secretly been made by the latter to the EM-
PEROR of MOROCCO, to farm his ports of *Tetuan, Tangier,*
and *Larache,* with a view of depriving the Garrison of
Gibraltar of any supplies from that quarter. This conduct
seemed to argue a confidence, that the mediation of Spain
would be rejected ; and it furnished the most unequivocal
proof, that that mediation was interposed, merely that its
rejection might furnish a feeble pretext for the commencement of hostilities against Great Britain. The EMPEROR
of MOROCCO, very fortunately, would not accede to the
proposal of farming his ports, though from the closeness
of the succeeding blockade, the Garrison derived from Barbary very slender and uncertain supplies.

The Rock of Gibraltar runs from North to South, pro-
jecting into the sea several miles from the Continent, to
which it is connected, as has been before described, by an
Isthmus of low sand. It is a part of the Province of Andalusia in Spain. From the perpendicular front to the
North, which is of various heights, to the Southernmost
point, which is called *Europa Point,* the distance is 2350
fathoms, or something more than two miles and a half.
The base of the Rock on the North front is 475 toises, or
950 yards, and the extreme breadth, taking it from the
New Mole to the Mediterranean side, is 800 toises, or 1600
yards. It is inaccessible for the whole length of its escarpment on the East, or Mediterranean side, which is called
the Back of the Rock. The North front, perpendicular
towards the Isthmus, is equally inaccessible, and the edge
of this perpendicular escarpment is occupied by twelve
Batteries commanding the Isthmus. The front to the •
West, and the Bay, is a gradual slope, and almost generally

of

of easy access. There are several roads on that side the Rock, which render the communication with the higher parts so easy, that cannon can be dragged up with the greatest facility. All these communications are open, and without retrenchments, except that part of the Lines which flanks the entrance to Land-Port and the Inundation. It is at the foot of this accessible slope, that the Town and Garrison are placed. The Town is closed, on the side of the Bay, by an irregular long wall, the defences of which are so inconsiderable as to admit of easy approach. The flanks, in short, are not by any means proportioned to the line of defence.

From the Town to the New Mole there is but little disputable ground. Between the New Mole and Europa Point, there are several accessible places, where an Enemy may land, and where some hundreds of men may form, without being immediately dislodged; a circumstance which would consequently create a considerable diversion in the Garrison. But these walls and lodgements are washed by the sea, which greatly protects them. This front indeed is so vulnerable, that it belies the commonly received idea of the impregnability of the Rock, which its general appearance to the eye so naturally suggests.

There are two ways of entering the Town from the Isthmus, one under the escarpments on the Cause-way, the other, under those of the Lines, which lead to the Glacis that covers the low front, presenting a curtain with two half bastions, on which are mounted twenty-six pieces of heavy Artillery, besides the protection already mentioned, of the flanking lines.

To

To the South, the Town is terminated by a retrenchment flanked by a bastion on the West side, a flat bastion
in the center, and a demi-bastion which commands both.
The post of Wind-Mill-Hill possesses several local advantages, of which sufficient avail has never yet been taken.

The first intimation that the Garrison had of the approaching Rupture betwixt Great Britain and Spain, was
on the 19th of June, 1779, from Mr. LOGIE, HIS MA-
JESTY's Consul in Barbary, who came over from Tangier
in a Swedish frigate, to apprize the Governor of the circumstance. He had learnt from a Swedish brig, that on
her passage to Tangier, she had fallen in with the French
Fleet consisting of about twenty eight sail of the line, cruiz-
ing off Cape Finisterre, in the expectation of being joined
by a Spanish Squadron from Cadiz. Only two days after
this it was, that the usual communication with the Spaniards was, on their part, put an end to.

At this juncture the strength of the Garrison consisted
of 5382 Men, inclusive of Officers; and of 663 serviceable pieces of Artillery.

From the previous prudence and attention of General
ELIOTT, and Lieutenant-General BOYD, few preparations remained to be made for the defence of the Garrison.
These able and judicious Officers had each, during their
respective commands, done every thing that military skill
and mature judgment could suggest; the chief object of
their present care, therefore, was the regular supply of fresh
provisions from Barbary, and in what manner the correspondence between Gibraltar and England was to be conducted.

ducted. Mr. Logie's presence in Barbary was very essential to the execution of both these objects; he therefore returned to Tangier on the 22d, having concerted with the Governor proper Signals, by which he might communicate intelligence across the Straits.

Admiral Duff, who commanded the British Squadron in the Mediterranean, removed the men of war from their usual anchorage, off Water-Port, where they were liable to be annoyed by the Enemy's Forts to the Southward, off the New Mole. His force at that time consisted of the *Panther* of sixty guns, the flag-ship, commanded by Captain Harvey; three frigates, two of which were on a cruise, and a sloop of war.

In consequence of the conduct of the Spaniards, new arrangements were made in the military detail of the Garrison. The Northern Guards were reinforced, and the picquets cautioned to be alert. Land-Port barriers were shut, and every step was taken which prudence required.

At the time that the communication with the Garrison was interdicted by the Spaniards, several Officers of the former were in the country upon parties of curiosity and pleasure. These were denied permission to return, but were conducted to Cadiz, or had pass-ports granted them to quit the kingdom by other routes. Three Officers, however, Colonel Ross, and Captain Vignoles of the 39th Regiment, and Captain Lefanue of the 56th, contrived to join their Corps, by assuming disguises, and risking the passage in a row-boat from Faro (a port in
Por-

Portugal) to Gibraltar. Others, in similar attempts, were unfortunately intercepted by the Enemy.

The Spaniards began to discover their future intentions by their movements in the Lines. All their Troops were employed in drawing down cannon from St. Roque, &c. to *animate* their Forts, and in using other means of strengthening their posts.

In the Garrison, mean while, every preparation was making to stand a vigorous Siege. No additional force to the usual Peace Establishment of the Spaniards appeared in the neighbourhood of the Rock, till the afternoon of the 5th of July, when a Spanish Squadron of two seventy-four gun ships, five frigates, and other vessels, to the number of eleven, hove in sight from the Westward, and lay-to for some time off the Garrison. At the same time three privateer cutters, under English Colours, came in from the Westward. A schooner, under Portuguese Colours, stood across from the Enemy to reconnoitre the first that came in, and on her return, she was fired upon from Europa Batteries, which was the first hostile shot from Gibraltar. In the evening the Enemy's Squadron drove to the Eastward, and on the 8th, it stood out of the Mediterranean, under an easy sail.

On the following day, the 6th of July, a packet was received from England, by the way of Lisbon and Faro, informing the Governor that Hostilities had commenced betwixt Great Britain and Spain. A Proclamation was made on the same evening, authorizing the capture of all

Spa-

Spanish Vessels, &c. and Letters of Marque for that purpose were granted to the Privateers in the Bay.

On the 16th the Enemy blocked up the Port of Gibraltar, with a Squadron of men of war, consisting of
two seventy-four gun ships, two frigates, five xebecs,
and a number of gallies, half-gallies, and armed settees.
They anchored in the Bay, off Algeziras, and keeping a
vigilant look-out, the Garrison became closely block-
aded.

On the 21st of this month, orders were issued for the
Troops to mount guard with their hair unpowdered, a
circumstance in itself apparently trifling, but which afterwards proved to be of great importance, and which was
strongly characteristic of the comprehensive and anticipa-
tive prudence of the General's mind.

In the course of the 22d, several Spanish Officers,
attended by a party of men, were observed tracing out
ground on the plain below St. Roque, apparently for
a Camp; and it was remarked that the Miquelets in the
advanced huts on the neutral ground, were relieved by Regular Troops. These Miquelets are of the same de-
scription with our Revenue Officers, and were stationed
on the Isthmus to prevent the smuggling of Tobacco into
Spain.

On the 26th the Enemy began to form a Camp on the
Plain below St. Roque, about half a mile from Point
Mala, and three miles from the Garrison. Fifty Tents
were pitched, and a detachment of Cavalry and Infantry

soon

soon after took possession, and reinforcements were thereafter daily pouring in.

The utmost activity now reigned in the Garrison, which
was not a little promoted by the Governor himself, who
was always present upon the parade by dawn of day, and
visited in person every part of the Works. Different parties were employed in not only further improving these,
complete as they already were, but in the erection of new
ones; and every precaution was used to weaken, and remedy
the effect of a general bombardment from the Enemy,
whenever that should take place.

The operations of the Spaniards, which had been unremitting, now began to attract the attention of the Governor. On the 11th of September a Council of War
was summoned to confer on the line of conduct to be
pursued. It consisted of the GOVERNOR, LIEUTENANT
GOVERNOR, Vice-Admiral DUFF, Major General De
la MOTTE; Colonels ROSS, GREEN, and GOODWIN,
with Sir THOMAS RICH, Bart. Commander of the *Enterprize* frigate. The result of this Council was made
known next morning, Sunday, September the 12th, by
the Artillery Officers being ordered to the Batteries on
the Heights, and these immediately opening on the Enemy's Works. Their advanced guards and workmen were
quickly forced to retire, and a general panic seemed to
have seized the whole Camp of the Enemy, for not a
man for several hours was to be seen within the range of
the Garrison guns.

In the beginning of October, the Spanish Army
amounted to about 14,000 men. Lieut. General Don
MARTIN

MARTIN ALVAREZ de SOTA MAYOR, was the Commander in Chief.

Several desertions had taken place from the Garrison since the commencement of the Siege, which were chiefly distressing on account of the intelligence which the Enemy might thence receive of the state of the provisions. It had hitherto seemed their object to starve the Garrison into a surrender.

The Enemy, mean while, kept busily employed in their Lines, notwithstanding the constant annoyance which they met with from the Garrison. By the 20th of this month no less than thirty-five embrasures were opened in their Lines, forming three Batteries; two of fourteen guns each, bearing on the Garrison Lines, and *Willis's,* and one of seven, apparently for the Town and Water-Port. They were cut through the parapet of their glacis, and situated between the Barrier of the Lines and Fort St. Philip. The Governor ordered the Artillery to direct their fire to these Works, and on the Seven Gun Battery in particular, where they had a party finishing what had been left imperfect in the night.

To follow the Besiegers and Besieged through all their succeeding operations, would far exceed the limits of the present Work. It must suffice, therefore, to narrate the principal occurrences only previous to the celebrated *Sortie.*

The Spaniards continued industriously to complete their Works, and the Garrison were equally indefatigable in annoying them, by a spirited, and well-directed fire. That varied as occasion seemed to demand, the Governor at all

times

times enforcing the strictest œconomy in the expenditure of the Stores.

By the month of November the Garrison began to be considerably distressed for provisions, a circumstance that seemed to have a very sensible effect upon the minds of all. Fresh provisions were beyond the reach of the generality of the Troops, mutton selling for three shillings, and three shillings and six-pence per pound ; veal for four shillings, pork for two shillings, and two shillings and six-pence; ducks from fourteen shillings to eighteen shillings a couple; and a goose a guinea : and the unfortunate Inhabitants were not, in general, so well off as the Troops, who had their scanty supply from the Garrison Stores at all times to depend upon.

Desertions were not unfrequent from the Enemy to the Garrison, by which means the Governor was apprized of all the proceedings in their Camp. On the other hand, some few of the Garrison, at different times, forsook their post, and went over to the Enemy. From the information conveyed by these Deserters, of the great scarcity of provisions in the Garrison, and the actual distress to which many were thereby subjected, the Enemy no doubt, flattered themselves that they should reduce the place by famine. They continued occasionally to fire upon the Town ; and in the beginning of January, 1780, intelligence was received by the Deserters, that they were making dispositions in their Lines for a general Bombardment. The alarm which this information spread amongst the Inhabitants was great ; but the Garrison, from some preparatory symptoms in the orders issued by the Admiral to the Squadron, began to entertain the

flattering

flattering hope that a Fleet of Relief was not far distant, and which pleasing idea made them more indifferent to the dispositions of the Enemy. In this hope of relief they were happily not disappointed, for, on the 19th of January, Sir GEORGE BRIDGES RODNEY entered the Straits, with a Squadron of twenty-one ships of the line, having under his convoy a very numerous Fleet of store-ships and victuallers.

The Plan for the Relief of Gibraltar had been conceived with a degree of secrecy and prudence, highly creditable to the British Ministry. The Enemy had imagined, by the intelligence which they received, that Sir GEORGE was to convoy the Fleet of Relief only to a certain latitude, from which he was to take his departure for the West-Indies, and leave his Convoy to their fate. Agreeable to this intelligence, the Spaniards had detached from their Grand Fleet, a Squadron, consisting only of eleven ships, with which they doubted not to intercept the whole of the Gibraltar Convoy.

On the 16th, at two P. M. Sir GEORGE RODNEY's Fleet got sight of the Spanish Squadron, and instantly gave chace. Cape St. Vincent then bore N. E. distant only four leagues. Some of the English men of war at four P. M. brought the Spaniards to action, which the former maintained with invincible spirit, upon a lee-shore, and during a very boisterous and squally night, till two o'clock in the morning, when the Spanish Admiral DON JUAN de LANGARA y HUARTE, with three others of his Squadron, was taken, one was run a-shore, and another blown up in the engagement. The rest saved themselves by flight.

In

In narrating a transaction so honourable to the British Flag, it cannot be deemed wholly foreign to the subject, to pay a passing tribute of respect to the Memory of an Officer now unfortunately no more, who contributed, in no inconsiderable degree, to the glorious issue of this fortunate rencontre. Captain YOUNG of the *Sandwich*, the Commander in Chief's Flag Ship, acted upon this occasion, during the indisposition of the Admiral, with a degree of spirit and judgment, which with all the Officers of the Fleet at that time gained him no small degree of credit; and which ought not to pass without the grateful remembrance of his countrymen. The signals were flying on board of the *Sandwich* for a pursuit of the Enemy, and for battle, and without timidly weighing the *dangers of a lee-shore*, he ran his ship into the thickest of the action, during which her bottom was sometimes within a very few feet of the ground. Such was the spirit which animated a HAWKE, and first established the glorious pre-eminence of the British Flag! Such *is* the spirit which alone can support it!

Sir GEORGE RODNEY having successfully relieved the Garrison, immediately proceeded to his destined command in the West Indies. While he remained in the Mediterranean, the Enemy's ships were blocked up at Algeziras, but as soon as the British Fleet re-passed the Straits, they resumed their station in the Bay, and recommenced the Blockade.

The Garrison was reinforced by the second Battalion of the 73d, or Lord MACLEOD's Regiment of Highlanders, commanded by Lieut. Colonel GEORGE MACKENZIE. This Regiment was intended for Minorca, but the Governor,

vernor, with the advice of the Admirals, thought it expedient to detain them.

The Garrison was now in a very perfect state of defence, and satisfaction was diffused through every bosom, at the liberality of the supplies which they had received from England, and the late important reinforcement to their strength.

Admiral Duff having returned to England in the Fleet which was sent home with the Spanish Prizes, the command of the Navy devolved on Captain Elliot, of the *Edgar*, who, on the 14th of February, hoisted a Broad Pendant as *Commodore*.

Desertions from the Spanish Camp became more and more frequent, and while the British Fleet remained in the Mediterranean, their distress, from the want of provisions, was little inferior to what the Garrison themselves had so recently experienced.

On the 27th of February, a Spanish Squadron of four line of battle ships, two frigates, and a xebec, joined Admiral Barcelo ; and on the 3d of March, a Spanish Convoy, under a Commodore, arrived in the Bay from the Westward.

From the time that the Enemy had sat down before the Rock, they had been unremittingly employed in forming depôts of earth, sand, and fascines, of which they constructed, on the glacis of the Lines, additional Mortar-Batteries.

On

On the 20th of April the *Edgar*, Commodore ELLIOT, sailed out to the Westward, notwithstanding the Enemy's superiority in the Bay.

In the beginning of June Mr. LOGIE intimated to the Commanding Naval Officer, that the Enemy had prepared several fireships, for the purpose of burning the English Men of War in the Bay. Early on the Morning of the 7th of this month they attempted to put their design in execution, but which was happily frustrated by the vigilance and intrepidity of the British Seamen. In their boats they grappled the fireships, nine in number, and towed them clear of their own vessels, under the walls of the Garrison, where the flames were extinguished.

The Isthmus which separates the Rock of Gibraltar from the Continent of Spain, is formed by sands thrown up by the Mediterranean Sea. It is not an improbable conjecture, that a regular chain of rock extended from the Mountain distinguished by the name of the Queen of Spain's Chair, to the Rock of Gibraltar, which by having been broken off and sunk in some violent convulsion of nature, has left to the North front of the Rock its present perpendicular and formidable appearance. This opinion is confirmed by the nature of the Isthmus, the foundation of which is most likely of uneven rock, and was at one period, probably covered by the sea; the present banks of sand of which the surface consists, have doubtless been thrown up by the strong flux and reflux of the Mediterranean Ocean. This opinion is further confirmed by the Devil's Tower being built upon a rock, which rises above the sand at a distance of 66 toises, or 132 yards from the base of the Rock of Gibraltar.

This

This Isthmus is traversed by a parallel, known by the name of the Spanish Lines, which were erected in 1733. This parallel is flanked to the West on the Bay side by Fort St. Phillip, and to the East, on the Mediterranean, by that of St. Barbara, embracing a space of 950 toises, or 1900 yards. From Fort St. Philip to the Rock of Gibraltar, the distance is 1000 toises, or 2000 yards. It was agreed by Convention, that the Spaniards should erect these Lines, to prevent Contraband Trade, and that the intervening Isthmus should be considered as neutral ground. On this neutral ground there are two Towers, which appear to have been the work of the Moors. One, near the Rock, is called the Devil's Tower; and the other, which is considerably larger, the Mill Tower, situated at the distance of 641⅓ toises, or 1286 yards from the North Battery, and from the salient angle of Fort St. Philip 466⅔ toises, or 936 yards.

Little of importance had been transacted by the Enemy, on the land side, till the 1st of October, when at day light it was observed they had raised an Epaulement, advanced from the center of their lines 300 toises, or 600 yards. During the preceding night, the out-guards of the Garrison had been alarmed with an unusual noise on the neutral ground, like that of men at work; several large fires were also seen, and some attempts were made to burn the advanced barriers, with devils and other combustibles, which, however, were thrown off without damage. As the morning advanced, the noise ceased, and when day light served, the above-mentioned Work appeared.

This Epaulement was about 30 yards in extent, of a simple construction, composed of chandeliers, fascines,

and

and a few sand-bags. Its situation was near the Windmill, or Tower, on the neutral ground, 1286 yards distant, as has been described, from the grand Battery of the Garrison. In the morning the Enemy's Guns were elevated, and their Batteries manned, ready to open upon the Rock, from the apprehension, probably, that the Garrison meant to fire upon their new work, and oppose the prosecution of it. These appearances probably induced the Governor to seem to disregard it during the day, but at night some light balls were thrown, to discover if they were making any additions to it. This advanced Work of the Enemy threw the Inhabitants into the utmost alarm and consternation : most of them retired to the Southward, apprehensive of a Bombardment.

From this new plan, thus begun to be carried into execution by the Enemy, it seemed that they meant to attempt a more vigorous attack, should their hopes from the Blockade be ultimately frustrated; but this first operation of erecting a Work so distant from, and unconnected with their Lines, contrary to every established mode of regular approach, created no small degree of surprize and speculation.

In the afternoon of the following day, Don ALVAREZ, acccompanied by Count D'ESTAING, visited the Lines. The Enemy did not appear eager to complete their Epaulement, but were employed in raising and finishing the Merlons of the Batteries in the Lines, and erecting a new Battery near the Guard-house on the beach, to the West, and in the Rear of Fort St. Philip, about 300 fathom distant from it; which Battery was afterwards called, by the Garrison, the *Black Battery*, and was supposed to have
been

been suggested by Count D'ESTAING from its being erected at the time he visited the Spanish Camp. This Battery enfiladed almost all the Line of Defence of the Garrison, on the Bay-side, and did otherwise a great deal of mischief to several flanks and other Batteries in the way of it. On the 14th it was completed, and the Artillery carried in.

At this period the Scurvy began to make dreadful ravages in the Garrison, from salt provisions having for some time been their only support. By the vigilance of the Enemy's Cruizers, they were cut off from all supplies from Barbary, and from Minorca these were comparatively trifling and uncertain.

In the night of the 21st, the Enemy threw up sand in the front of their Epaulement, to cover it against the fireballs and carcasses from the Garrison. On the 26th they lengthened it to the west about 30 yards, and strengthened it in front with sand. During the night of the 28th, they erected two large traverses in the rear for magazines. The whole now presented a very compact appearance, and it was concluded that it was intended for a Mortar Battery.

In the beginning of November, the Governor made an arrangement of the Troops, that in case the Enemy should bombard the Garrison, each Regiment should know the particular quarters and post which it should occupy. The fire from the Rock on the 7th and 8th of this month, became more animated, notwithstanding which the Enemy, almost every night, made some interior additions to their Work. In the evening of the 10th, a large party, followed

G   by

by a number of carts and mules, laden with different materials, advanced along the beach, from the Sally-Port of
the ditch of Fort St. Philip to the Mill-Battery, by which
name the advanced work of the Spaniards was now distinguished. They were observed by the Artillery at *Willis's*
before they got half way, and a brisk *ricochetting* fire was
opened upon them, which threw them into confusion. The
Batteries being reinforced, the firing was continued with
great vivacity the whole night. The same annoyance of
them was continued on subsequent nights, but they persevered, notwithstanding the great losses they must have
sustained, till a line of communication with their Batteries
was completed.

During the night of the 17th, the Enemy threw up two
Places d'Armes for musquetry, on the flanks of the Mill-
Battery: the parapets formed semicircles joining the
Battery, but afterwards extended in an oblique direction
towards the Lines. These additions appeared very slight,
being only a row of casks or gabions, strengthened with
half-chandeliers and sand in front, covered on the top with
sand-bags.

The Gun-boats of the Enemy now began to be very
troublesome to the Garrison, as they had been considerably
increased in point of number.

On the 22d a great number of mules were employed in
carrying forward casks, chandeliers, and other materials
from the Camp; and in the night of the 23d, the Enemy
began an approach from the Lines to the Mill-Battery. It
consisted of fascines, with sand banked up in front, and
commenced near the west angle of the Western Fourteen
Gun

Gun Battery, extending about 120 feet towards the advanced Guard-house in front of Fort. St. Philip; on the following night they lengthened it about 100 feet, with chandeliers placed in a trench, and filled with faccines.

Notwithstanding the weather in the month of December was extremely unfavourable, from violent rains, the Spaniards did not at all remit in their labours. On the 14th they had joined the fourth branch of approach to the extremity of the eastern *Place d'Armes*, and two nights following began a fifth branch, which by the 19th was extended to the east of the Mill-Battery. During this period they had likewise erected a Mortar Battery for the sea, to the north of Fort St. Barbara; and large and small traverses were raised within both Forts, to protect their men from the upper batteries of the Garrison. Their advanced Works being completed, to their Centre Battery, which from its extent, height and solidity, was evidently intended for mortars, the Spaniards gave the name of *St. Carlos*.

Early in January, 1781, Consul LOGIE, with his family and all the British Subjects who had been resident in Barbary, arrived at Gibraltar. The EMPEROR of MOROCCO having been been disappointed in some Presents which he expected from Great Britain, and having received fresh offers from the Spanish Court, to induce him to abandon the interests of the English, he at length consented, and became wholly subservient to the hostile wishes of the Spaniards towards all those of the English Nation who were settled in Barbary. He began to shew his change of sentiments, by treating the British Consul with every species of indignity, and even authorizing towards him and the other

British

British Subjects in his dominions, the greatest violence and outrage. This Mr. LOGIE bore with a manly fortitude, from the hope that his residence in Barbary might still be of service to the Garrison of Gibraltar ; but the EMPEROR at length avowed, that he had sold the port of *Tangier* to the KING of SPAIN, and issued an order for every Christian, but of that Nation, to quit the Town and Bay by the 1st of January, 1781. In violation of this Edict, however, Mr. LOGIE learnt, on the 26th, of December, that the EMPEROR had given up all the British Subjects as prisoners to the Spaniards. Mr. LOGIE, with several others, was conducted to Algeziras, from whence, after being detained there for several days, he was sent over to Gibraltar.

The arrival of Vice Admiral DARBY's Fleet in the Straits, on the 12th of April, 1781, excluded every hope of reducing the Garrison by famine, as it introduced a Convoy of Victuallers amply provided with good and wholesome provisions.

The anchoring of His Majesty's Ship the *Edgar* off the Old Mole, seemed to serve as the signal for the immediate commencement of a most furious cannonade and bombardment, from every piece of ordnance the Besiegers could bring to bear upon the place. The havock and ruin caused among the houses by this formidable fire, obliged the Garrison and Inhabitants immediately to retire to the southward, the Military Corps to the ground marked out for their respective Encampments, and the Inhabitants to hide themselves in gullies, crannies and caves, at the greatest possible distance from the usual range of the Enemy's shot and shells. The Town was soon reduced to one confused mass

of

of rubbish, and a very small portion of the Garrison had any other protection against the weather or the Enemy's fire, besides the canvas of their tents.

The landing of the Stores and Provisions, which was performed under the inspection of Rear Admiral Sir JOHN LOCKHART ROSS, whom Admiral DARBY had sent in with six sail of the line for that purpose, was much incommoded by the Enemy's Gun-boats. These attacked the Fleet regularly every morning when it was calm. The Rear Admiral, however, whose spirit and vigilance were not to be surpassed, kept a constant guard of ships and frigates under sail, to protect the vessels at anchor from 16 fire-ships that were lying at Algeziras, ready to be used the first fair opportunity.

On the 20th, the supplies being landed, Sir JOHN LOCKHART ROSS weighed with his Squadron, and joined Admiral DARBY, who immediately, the wind being fair, stood out to the westward.

It was not till the 23d, that the Bombardment abated, in consequence of the Batteries on the Spanish Lines having been shaken and injured by their own unremitting Cannonade. It was computed, that, during this Bombardment, no less than 200 shot and shells were, upon an average, thrown into the Garrison every hour. The effect of the Enemy's fire upon the Works of the Garrison was very considerable, but that was soon remedied by the vigilance and assiduity of the Engineers. The casualties, however, in consequence of their fire, were very numerous.

The

The Bombardment on the part of the Enemy confi-
nued, with occasional variations, and their Gun-boats
were regular in their nightly visits, harrassing the Garrison, and sometimes doing a considerable deal of damage.

In the month of September, the Spaniards began to
make some additions to their advanced Works. During
the night of the 15th of that month, they threw up three
banks of sand in *zig-zags*, beginning at the centre of the
fourth branch of approach, which seemed intended as a
line of direction for a new communication to the St.
Carlos's Battery. On the 19th they *debouched* the fourth
branch of the approach about the centre.

On the 1st of October, the Anniversary of the Commencement of the St. Carlos's Battery, the Spaniards began to construct St. Paschal's Battery, to the west of
the Mill Town, near the extremity of the last line of
approach. On the 4th they made an obtuse angle from
the west to the new line of Gabions towards the North,
and constructed a communication from its eastern extremity to the Powder Magazine of the Mill-Battery. During the night of the 5th they drew a line reaching from
the angle of the fourth and fifth lines of approach, towards the east, about twelve toises in length. On the
6th they continued working on St. Paschal's Battery, and
had lengthened the Eastern Line about sixteen fathoms.
On the 8th they lengthened the Eastern Line, and turned
it more towards the Devil's Tower, forming an angle.
On the 18th, a mortar was perceived in St. Paschal's
Battery. During the night of the 19th they made a battery for six guns, west of the angle formed by the first

and

and second lines of their communication from the centre of the fourth line of approach.

On 2d of November the Enemy made two excavations, one in the rear of the new Mortar, and other in the rear of the Mill-Battery; the borders of which were framed in by large square pieces of timber, and lined inside with fascines. These excavations were about five feet deep, and were naturally supplied with two feet of water. On the 5th they began to form an Epaulement in the rear of the West Epaulement of their new Gun Battery. On the 12th they began another Battery for six guns, more to the West than the former, and to the rear of it, but did not quite complete it, joining at right angles with the Epaulement above mentioned.

The firing from the Rock was regularly kept up during the night at this period, in order to annoy the Enemy in the prosecution of their Works, and they generally returned the fire with considerable vivacity.

Notwithstanding the Enemy were so much exposed in their Works to the fire of the Garrison, they continued with astonishing spirit and exertion to bring them to a completion. One of the new Batteries to the right of St. Carlos was to contain six heavy cannon, fixed in their platforms at a great elevation, according to the Spanish term, *d'empotrada* (propt up), or raised to an elevation of forty-five degrees, for the purpose of harrassing the British Soldiers in their Camp, by keeping up a continual and successive fire of dropping shot both by day and night.

The

The Garrison had, from long habitude, by this time become inured to every species of danger and fatigue. They had hitherto braved the hardships of the Siege with unparalleled firmness and alacrity, animated by the noble consciousness of fighting for the Honour of their Country. For a series of several months, they had not enjoyed above one night's uncertain repose in three, to refit them for the arduous duties of their several stations. The British and Hanoverian Soldiers, however, though unaccustomed to shrink from danger, to repine at hard fare, or complain of excessive labour, could not bear the idea of being perpetually exposed to the Enemy's fire, even in the hour of repose, and of necessary relaxation from the fatigues of duty. This reflection began to make a sensible and melancholy impression upon the minds of the Soldiery, and became the object of serious attention with the Governor, ever alive to the voice of complaint, and ever vigilant in his designs upon the Enemy. It became his anxious wish to remove the cause of apprehension in his Garrison, before it could be realized, by the opening of the Battery *d'empotrada* upon the Camp.

The Spaniards had now been employed nearly thirteen months on their advanced Works. The nature of the soil, and the downward fire from the Garrison, by whom all their operations were seen, rendered their progress laborious, tedious, and dangerous. It was impossible to sink the Trench in the sand, under which they found water at the depth of three feet.

It was therefore necessary to construct all these Works with an enormous quantity of chandeliers, and large

beams

beams in the form of frames, and with a vast number of fascines and sand-bags. They at length completed, however, this formidable front, the *Epaulements* of which were twenty-two feet high, defended by several flanks. These communications, together with an infinite number of traverses, and three large Powder Magazines, they constructed under an unremitting fire from the Garrison, with unexampled coolness and perseverance.

The Army of the Besiegers was now 14,000 strong, and their ordnance pointed against the Garrison formidable in the extreme. It may not be unsatisfactory here to recapitulate it.

Number of Ordnance in the Spanish Works and Lines
during the Blockade, at the time of the Sortie.

GUNS WITHIN THE LINES.

Guns.

Fort St. Philip, - - - - - - 24
La Infanta, - - - - - - - 7
La Princessa, - - - - - - - 14
El Principe, - - - - - - - 14
Fort St. Barbara, - - - - - - 24

GUNS BEHIND THE LINES.

Batteria del Rey, to the N. W. of Fort St. Philip, - 10

GUNS IN THE ADVANCED WORKS.

St. Martin's, West of the Mill Tower, - - 12
St. Pasquale, S. W. of ditto. - - - - 6

In all, - - - - - - 101

MORTAR BATTERIES.

WITHIN THE LINES.

No. 1. On the Covered Way of the East Angle
of Fort St. Philip, - - - } - 4
2. On the ditto, joining ditto with the Lines - - 7
3. On the West Face of the *Place à l'Armes*
at the re-entering Angle of the two Batteries La Princessa and El Principe, - } - 5
4. On the second *Place d'Armes*, - - - 5
5. Near the centre of the Communication
to the third *Place d'Armes* - - } - 4

IN THE ADVANCED WORKS.

St. Carlos, or Mill-Battery, 13-inch Sea Mortars - 8
St. Paschal's · ditto, ditto - - 2
To the West of Fort St. Philip, behind the Lines,
at the foot of the Glacis - - - } - 5
On the Rear of Fort St. Barbara, - - - - 4

44

In all, 155 Pieces of Ordnance.

About this time, information from various quarters uniformly concurred in assuring the General, that the Enemy, considering the Garrison as few in number, debilitated by the scurvy, and wearied out with fatigue, concluded that the British Soldiers were not in a condition for active enterprize ; and laying aside, therefore, every apprehension of danger to their Works from that quarter, gave themselves up to a degree of listlessness and indolence, perfectly inconsistent with the first principles of Military Discipline.

On the Evening of the 20th of November, two Deserters from the Walloon Guards came in at Land-Port, and were immediately conducted to the Governor's Head-Quarters. One of them was a Corporal, a shrewd intelligent fellow. He was a man of such observation as to be perfectly versed in the detail and disposition of the Enemy's Works, Guards, and Forts.

He brought with him a rough sketch of the advanced Works, drawn by himself, with a common pen, upon the spot, but sufficiently correct to convey a satisfactory idea of them, and to elucidate his own deposition, which was that night taken down by the Town-Major. It was so clear and distinct, that a correct Plan of the Spanish Camp, Night-Guards, and Out-Posts, from Algeziras to Fort Barbara, might have been made out from it. So well-informed was he, and so accurate in every thing he advanced upon that occasion, that he never once contradicted himself in the most trivial circumstance, through a continued series of cross-examination. This Deserter attended the Governor to *Willis's*, where he further described

scribed

scribed to him various parts of the Enemy's Works and Camp.

The perfect co-incidence of the various information which the Governor had, through different channels, obtained, describing the carelessness with which the night-duty was carried on in the Enemy's Camp and Works, suggested the idea of a *Sortie*, which under other circumstances could not have been hazarded, consistently with the safety of the Garrison.

There can be little doubt but General ELIOTT, ever since the apprehensions of the Soldiery reached his ear from the effect of the Battery *d'Empotrada*, had revolved in his mind the practicability of destroying these Works of the Enemy, and formed in secret that Plan, which he executed with the caution and firmness which so peculiarly characterized him. The present, from a fortunate concurrence of circumstances, seemed to be the opportunity the most favourable for carrying such a great and hazardous Enterprize into effect.

The Governor, therefore, having digested his Plan in his own capacious and enlightened mind, and having weighed every step that ought to be taken to insure success, committed to paper the necessary Instructions for the different Officers who were to be leading Agents in its execution.

Early in the afternoon of the 26th of November, all the houses where wine and spirits were retailed out to Soldiers, were shut up, to prevent every degree of intoxi-
cation

cation in the Garrison ; and, a little after sun-set, orders
were issued for a Detachment to parade at midnight on
the Red-Sands.   Mean while, all the General Officers
in the Garrison were summoned to attend the Governor
at the Field Officers' Room to the southward, where every
other Officer who was to be entrusted with any particular
command in this important Enterprize, was present. The
Governor then opened his design, read his Plan, and
gave his Instructions to the Executive Officers, who were
required to propose whatever alterations they thought
should be made in that part of the disposition which regarded their own command ; to many of which alterations
the Governor agreed, by this means rendering those
Gentlemen more particularly interested in the success of
the Enterprize.

(62)

The following is a Copy of the ORDERS issued upon
this Occasion.

EVENING GARRISON ORDERS.

Gibraltar, Nov. 26th, 1781.

Countersign, STEADY.

" All the Grenadiers and Light Infantry of the Gar-
" rison, and all the Men of the 12th, and HARDEN-
" BERG's Regiments, Officers and Non-Commissioned
" Officers, now on duty, to be immediately relieved, and
" to join their Regiments: to form a Detachment, con-
" sisting of the 12th, and HARDENBERG's Regiments
" complete; the Grenadiers and Light Infantry of all the
" other Regiments, (which are to be completed to their
" full Establishment from the Battalion Companies ;)
" one Captain, three Lieutenants, ten Non-Commis-
" sioned Officers, and a hundred Artillery; and three
" Engineers, seven Officers, and twelve Non-Commis-
" sioned Officers, Overseers ; with a hundred and sixty
" Workmen from the Line, (excepting the 12th and
" HARDENBERG's Regiments) and forty Workmen from
" the Artificer Company. Each man to carry thirty-six
" rounds of Ammunition, a good flint in his piece, and
" another in his pocket. No Drums to go out, except-
" ing two with each of the Regiments. No Volunteers
" to be allowed. The whole to assemble on the Red-
" Sands at twelve o'clock this night, and to be command-
" ed by Brigadier General Ross, for the purpose of making
" a *Sortie* upon the Enemy's Batteries. The 39th and
" 58th

" 58th Regiments to parade at the same hour on the Grand
" Parade, under the command of Brigadier General Pic-
" ton, to sustain the *Sortie* if neces sary."

All the Officers belonging to this Detachment, then on
guard, were immediately relieved, and every preparation
made enjoined in the Orders.

At the hour appointed, the whole Detachment was assembled at the place of rendezvous, and was joined by
one hundred Sailors, commanded by Lieutenants Muckle
and Campbell of the Navy. It was formed in three
lines, two deep.

The Right-Hand Line formed - - - the Rear.
The Centre - - - - - - - - the Centre
The Left-Hand - - - - - - - - the Front.

Disposition and Force of the Detachment.

Brigadier General Ross.

Left Column. Lieut. Col. Trigge.

	o.	s.	d.	r.&f.
72d Grenadiers	4	5	0	101
72d Light Infantry	4	5	0	101
Sailors, with an Engineer	3	3	0	100
Royal Artillery	1	4	0	35
12th Regiment	26	28	2	430
58th Light Infantry	3	3	0	57
	41	48	2	824

Centre Column. Lieut. Col. Dachenhausen. Major Maxwell. The Reserve.

	o.	s.	r.&f.
39th Grenadiers	3	3	57
39th Light Infantry	3	3	57
73d Grenadiers	4	5	101
73d Light Infantry	4	5	101
Engineer with workmen	6	14	150
Royal Artillery	2	4	40
56th Grenadiers	3	3	57
58th Grenadiers	3	3	57
	28	40	620

Right Column. Lieut. Col. Hugo.

	o.	s.	d.	r.&f.
Reden's Grenadiers	8	7	0	71
La Motte's Grenadiers	3	7	0	71
Engineer with workmen	4	6	0	50
Royal Artillery	1	2	0	25
Hardenberg's Regt.	16	34	2	296
56th Light Infantry	3	3	0	57
	30	59	2	570

GENERAL RETURN OF THE GARRISON

ON THE 26th OF NOVEMBER, 1781.

	Colonels	Lieut. Colonels	Majors	Captains	Lieutenants	Ensigns	Chaplains	Adjutants	Quarter-Masters	Surgeons	Mates	Serjeants	Drummers	Rank and File.	
Total out with the Sortie	1.	3.	3.	26.	60.	14.	0.	3.	0.	0.	2.	147.	4.	1914	exclusive of 100 Sailors,
Sick in Hospital	0.	0.	0.	0.	1.	1.	0.	0.	0.	0.	0.	28.	6.	557	
Remaining in Garrison	5.	5.	5.	45.	71.	31.	3.	7.	8.	9.	14.	266.	181.	2531.	
Total strength of the Garrison } before the Sortie	6.	8.	8.	72.	132.	46.	3.	10.	8.	9.	16.	441.	191.	5002.	Total strength 5952.

I

Tools of all kinds for demolishing the Enemy's Works were delivered to the Workmen, and the following directions for their destination communicated to the principal Officers :

" The Right Column to lead, and to march through
" FORBES's Barrier, for the extremity of the Parallel,
" keeping the eastern fences of the Gardens close on
" the left hand. The Centre immediately to follow,
" marching through Bay-side Barrier, and directing their
" course through the middle of the Gardens, to the
" object of their destination. The Left Column to fol-
" low the Centre through Bay-side Barrier, then to march
" to their destination, keeping the western fences of the
" Gardens on their right hand.

" When the Rear of the Right Column has got clear
" of FORBES's, and the Rear of the Left clear of Bay-
" side, the Heads of the Three Columns are, as much as
" circumstances will admit, to be found in a Line, and to
" march on so as to arrive at their different points of At-
" tack at the same time.

" No person to advance before the front on any pre ·
" tence whatever, unless commanded so to do by the Of-
" ficer leading the Column. The most profound silence
" to be observed, as the success of the Enterprize may
" depend thereon.

" The Troops of the Right Column, preceding the
" Workmen and Artillery, are destined to attack, and
" force the Eastern Parallel of the Enemy's Approaches.

" The

" The Troops of the Centre Column, preceding the
" Workmen and Artillery, are destined to attack and
" force the two Mortar Batteries.

" The Troops of the Left Column, preceding the
" Workmen and Artillery, are to attack and force the two
" Six-Gun Batteries. •

" The Troops appointed to each particular Attack are
" to form in a Line as soon as they arrive at a proper
" distance from the several objects, and as the ground
" will permit.

" The Workmen and Artillery are to form in Divi-
" sions.   The 12th, and HARDENBERG's Regiments,
" composing the Sustaining Corps, are to form in one
" Line to the front, and to be ready to detach to the right
" and left, as occasion may require.

" The Reserve, after having assisted in the Storm, and
" the Works are carried, to form in the farthest Gar-
" dens, at some distance in the Rear of the Sustaining
" Corps.   The Grenadiers of the 56th and 58th, in the
" Centre, the Light Company of the 56th fronting to
" the East ; and the Light Company of the 58th fronting
" to the West.

" As soon as the different Works are carried, the
" Troops that have performed these Services are to
" form, and take up their ground in the following man-
" ner, in order to cover their several Working Parties and
" Artillery :

" Of

" Of the Right Column, the Grenadiers of REDEN's
" and La MOTTE's, are to form behind the Parallel.

" Of the Centre Column, the Light Companies and
" Grenadiers of the 39th and 73d Regiments are to form
" along the front and communication of the fourth branch
" of Approach.

" Of the Left Column, the Grenadiers of the Light
" Company of the 72d Regiment are to post themselves
" behind the westernmost Six-Gun Battery, covering
" their Right Flank with the fourth long breach of Ap-
" proach, and with their left to the Gun Battery close to
" the Beach."

The point of Attack assigned to each Column, was
the precise spot where the Enemy's Guards were posted,
that the suddenness of the danger might put it out of
their power to reflect, and to take any defensive measures that might essentially retard the progress of the Assailants.

By the time the above Destination of the Columns was
made known to the different Officers, and other necessary
arrangements had taken place, the morning of the 27th
was pretty far advanced. At about a quarter before
three o'clock, the moon had nearly set, and that darkness
was coming on, indispensably necessary to the successful execution of the Enterprize. At this time it was that
the Detachment began its march, by files from the right
of the Rear Line, for the Attack. Although nothing
could exceed the order and silence of the Troops, when
the

the Right-Hand Column had got near the Gardens, they were three times challenged by one of the Enemy's advanced Sentries, but no answer being returned, he immediately fired at the Column, and retired some paces, when he fired a second shot. The Column kept moving forwards.——A second Sentry discharged his piece, and retired. Lieutenant Colonel Hugo, finding the Enemy alarmed, immediately formed the Attacking Corps, and pushed on for the Eastern Parallel. When they came near, a third Sentinel fired at them ; upon which the Grenadiers returned the fire, and leapt into the Works. The Enemy fled in that quarter, without attempting further opposition. The Workmen immediately began to dismantle that part of the Works, and the Artillery soon after set them on fire.

Part of HARDENBERG's Regiment, attached to this Column, owing to the darkness of the morning, found themselves with the Storming Party of the Centre Column, in front of the St. Carlos Battery. In this situation, immediately before the Centre of the Left Flank of the Battery, no alternative remained but pushing forward, which they did in the most gallant manner, receiving at the same time a discharge of three rounds of musquetry from the Enemy defending that Flank. Upon their mounting the Parapet, the Enemy precipitately gave way, when the Hanoverians, with considerable difficulty, descended the stupendous Work, forming with their left to the Tower. They were thus situated when Lieutenant Colonel DACHENHAUSEN, at the head of the 39th Flank Companies, got over the St. Carlos Battery, and naturally mistaking them for Spaniards, fired upon them, and wounded several. Further mischief was, however,

prevented

prevented by the *Countersign.* The Grenadiers of La
MOTTE's and REDEN's, after having stormed the Eastern Parallel, and dislodged the Enemy from the Centre
Guard-House, * formed in the Rear of the Parallel, fronting towards the Enemy's Lines.

The Centre Column was fired at as soon as it entered
the Gardens, and the Enemy's Out-Sentries continued
firing and retreating as it advanced. When the Column
had got near the St. Carlos Battery, a smart fire was for
a short time kept up by the Enemy from their Flanks, but
the Storming Party at the head of the Column, consisting of the 39th and 73d Flank Companies, with the 56th
and 58th Grenadiers, commanded by Lieutenant Colonel
DACHENHAUSEN, and Major MAXWELL, rushing forward, soon drove them from their Works. How to descend into the Battery now became a matter of some
difficulty; for from the scaffold on the inside to the platform of the Batteries, the height was eighteen feet, and
the Enemy had removed the steps or ladders by which
they mounted to the scaffold. Some of the most active of
the British having leaped down upon the sand, their Com-
rades followed the example, and they were immediately
masters of the Work.

The Left-Hand Column proceeded according to instructions, and possessed themselves of the Two-Gun
Batteries without much resistance, in which they took
prisoners several Spanish Grenadiers. Such were the spirit

---

* There were three Guard Houses upon the Isthmus, built of stone.
One near the Mill-Tower, called the Centre Guard-House, one to the
right upon the Bay, and a third to the left on the Mediterranean.

rit and activity with which Lieutenant Colonel TRIGGE, at the head of the 58th Light Infantry, and the Flank Companies of the 72d Regiment, pushed on to the Two-Gun Batteries on the side of the Bay, that the Enemy were incapable of making any resistance, but fled with the greatest precipitation; and several Spanish Grenadiers were afterwards taken prisoners in their splinter-proofs, where they had been asleep when the British Troops entered the Batteries. All their Batteries were constructed with slinter-proofs capable of containing a very great number of men.

The Sailors belonging to the Left Column, to be employed as Workmen, mistook their way, and made for the Mortar-Batteries, so that the Gun-Batteries were not destroyed as soon as the others: but this mistake being rectified, the Seamen proceeded to demolish them with an increased impetuosity, and the Batteries were speedily on fire.

The ardour of the Assailants was irresistible. The Enemy on all sides fled, abandoning with the utmost precipitation those Works, which it had cost them so much labour, and so much blood and treasure to erect.

When the British Troops had taken possession, the Attacking Corps formed, agreeably to their orders, to repel any attempt which the Enemy might make to prevent the total destruction of their Works, whilst the 12th Regiment took post in front of the St. Carlos Battery, to sustain the Western Attack; and the Reserve, under Major MAXWELL, drew up in the Gardens nearest the Spanish Works.

The

The 12th Regiment and HARDENBERG's were drawn up with considerable intervals between the Companies, that the Artificers and Pioneers might retire between the intervals, in case of being forced back, and that their retreat might be thus effected without loss or confusion.

Captain CURTIS, Commander of the Squadron, went out in the *Sortie* as a Volunteer, and, with Lieutenants MUCKLE and CAMPBELL, under his command, led on the Volunteer Seamen. Such, indeed, was the general ardour to partake in this bold Enterprize, that every man considered himself as unfortunate, who was obliged to remain behind within the walls of the Garrison.

The exertions of the Seamen, Artillery, and Artificers, upon the Enemy's Works, were astonishing. The Batteries were soon in a state for the fire-faggots to operate, and the flames spread with astonishing rapidity into every part. The column of fire and smoke which rolled from the Works, grandly illuminated the Troops and neighbouring objects, forming altogether a *coup-d'œil,* which it is impossible by language to describe, and of which the Pencil of the Painter alone can convey an adequate idea.

Ten brass thirteen-inch Sea-Mortars, and eighteen brass twenty-six pounders were spiked by the Artillery-Men in the Enemy's Works. Amongst the latter were the six guns mounted *d'empotrada.* About the time that the fire was spreading along the Batteries, in spiking one of the Mortars in the St. Carlos Battery, an explosion took place, by which some of the Workmen were hurt.

In

In an hour, the object of the *Sortie* was fully effected, and trains being laid to the Magazines, Brigadier Ross ordered the Advanced Corps to withdraw, and the Sustaining Regiments to cover their retreat. They retired with the most perfect deliberation, and in the best order ; but, by some over-sight, the Barrier at FORBES's was locked after the Flank Companies had returned, which might have proved of serious consequences to HARDENBERG's Regiment, had the Enemy attempted to annoy the retreat, as the Hanoverians were obliged, from that circumstance, to follow the 12th Regiment through Bay-side. The whole Detachment had got back into the Town, in less than two hours from the time of its sally.

Several small quantities of powder took fire whilst the Detachment was on its retreat ; and just as the Rear had got within the Garrison, the principal Magazine blew up with a tremendous explosion, throwing up vast pieces of timber, which, falling into the flames, increased the general conflagration.

The British carried with them into the Garrison, nineteen Prisoners ; and themselves sustained no other loss than that of four Men killed, and one Officer and twenty-five others wounded : The following is a Copy of the Return delivered in to the General.

_____

K   *Return*

Return of the Killed, Wounded, and Missing.

Corps.	Killed.				Wounded.				Missing.	Remarks.
	Offrs.	Sergts.	Drums.	R. & F.	Offrs.	Sergts.	Drums.	R. & F.	R. & F.	
R. Artillery,	—	—	—	—	1	—	—	1	—	
18th Regt.	—	—	—	1	—	—	—	1	—	
89th ditto,	—	—	—	—	—	1	—	—	—	
72d ditto,	—	—	—	1	—	—	—	1	—	Lieut. Tweedie wounded
73d ditto,	—	—	—	—	—	—	—	2	1	
Soldier Artificers,	—	—	—	—	—	—	—	1	—	
Hardenberg's,	—	—	—	2	1	1	—	11	—	
Reden's,	—	—	—	—	—	—	—	—	—	
Seamen,	—	1	—	—	—	—	—	5	—	one only dangerously.
Total				4	1	2		22	1	

Lieutenant TWEEDIE received a grape shot in the thigh, immediately as the 12th Regiment had formed in front of the St. Carlos Battery. This gallant Officer, after having received the shot, which broke his thigh, supported himself, in his post, on the other knee and his spontoon, and in this position he was first discovered by General ELIOTT, as he was passing along the front of the Regiment.— The General asked him " why he was in that situation?" to which Mr. TWEEDIE coolly replied, " that he was wounded." The General immediately ordered him to be assisted, and conveyed to the Garrison, not without bestowing due praise upon his gallantry and resolution.

The only man of the Detachment who did not return into the Garrison, was a private of the 73d Grenadiers. This man was one of the first to mount the Battery, where he encountered with the Spanish Captain of Artillery whom he wounded, and by whom he was wounded in turn. The Soldier fell upon the top of the Battery, and when the Troops were ordered to retire, the flames spread with such rapidity to the spot where he lay, that it was impossible to save him. It is to be regretted that the name of this gallant Soldier cannot now be ascertained. It is worthy of being transmitted with honour to posterity, as an incitement to others in a similar situation to act with a heroism that would well adorn a higher rank.

Although the Enemy must have been early alarmed, not the smallest effort was made to save, or to avenge the destruction of their Works. The fugitives seemed to have communicated a panic to the whole; for their Army, though drawn out under arms in the front of their Camp, remained silent and inactive spectators of the Conflagration. Instead of materially annoying the British Detach-

ment

ment from the Flanking Forts, which might have been done with very great effect, they directed the fire from their Lines chiefly towards the Town and Upper Batteries, from whence a warm and well-served discharge of round shot was returned upon their Forts and Barrier. To the latter indeed, the fire from the Garrison was chiefly directed, to prevent the Camp from detaching any Troops to the support of the Party in the Advanced Works, which would have been thus rendered a service of very peculiar danger.

With respect to the number of the Enemy in their Advanced Batteries at the time of the *Sortie*, different statements have been made. It was a generally received opinion in the Garrison at the time, that the Spanish Guard consisted only of one Captain, three Subalterns, and seventy-four Privates, including the Artillery. Though even this small force, in such strong Works, might have kept any numbers at bay, till a reinforcement had been sent from the Lines, yet for the glory of the Enterprize, it becomes satisfactory to state, from the best authority, that the Enemy's force was much more considerable. The following Return was communicated some time afterwards by a Relation to the Commander in Chief of the Spanish Camp, and may be relied upon as authentic.

SPANISH GUARD IN THE ADVANCED WORKS.

One Company of Militia Grenadiers - - - 100
One ditto of Walloon Guards - - - 100
Three Companies of Artillery, of 70 men each 210

Total 410

When

When the extent of the Works is considered, with the numbers of Mortars and heavy Artillery which they contained, it is absurd to suppose that a much smaller number than the above could serve the Batteries, as the duty in them must have been extremely laborious, both Guns and Mortars being frequently discharged in vollies. It is hardly credible, that men should have been occasionally detached from the Lines for the performance of that duty, and then permitted to return; that would have been a practice inconsistent with the first principles of Military Service.

As a corroborating proof, that the above is an accurate Return of the Spanish Force in the Advanced Works, at the period of the *Sortie*, amongst the few Prisoners there were some of different Corps; of the Walloon Guards, Militia Grenadiers and Artillery. In the St. Carlos Battery alone, there was one Captain of Artillery killed, and a Lieutenant of that Corps, and a Captain, *en second*, of the Walloon Guards, were made Prisoners. This sufficiently proves, that there must have been a Company of Artillery, besides a Detachment of the Walloon Guards, and these had to serve eight thirteen-inch Sea Mortars, each of which would require at least fourteen men. It is to be concluded, that the other Batteries were occupied in an equal proportion.

The Lieutenant made prisoner was Don VINCENTE FRIZA. This Officer was taken in the middle of the Battery by Captain WITHAM of the Royal Artillery, who commanded the Detachment of that Corps out upon this service. The Spanish Officer was armed with a drawn sword, when Captain WITHAM, with a firebrand only in

his

his hand, seized him by the sword-arm, and in Spanish demanded the Key of the Magazine of that Battery. Don VINCENTE replied, " *Seignior, todos es Bombas*"——" the whole is a Magazine," and gave up his sword.

That the Spaniards never entertained the smallest apprehension of a *Sortie* from the Garrison, was evident from the circumstances in which they were found, for even four hundred Men were but a weak guard for Works of such importance and extent. The Chief Commandant of the Spanish Camp, too, was sleeping that night at St. Roque, two miles distant from his post; and in one of the splinter proofs of the Batteries was found the Report of the Commanding Officer, which, when the Guard was relieved, was to have been sent to the Spanish General. The Report expressed, " that nothing extraordinary had happened," which clearly evinces the unmilitary state of security in which the Spaniards conceived themselves to be.

It has since been learnt, from very unquestionable authority, that a Court Martial, by order of the Commander in Chief, sat upon the Commandant in the Spanish Lines. The former imputed the success of the *Sortie* to the negligence or want of conduct of the latter, in not permitting the Spanish Cavalry to go out of the Lines. The Field Officer who commanded there, and who was of the rank of Colonel, waited for orders from the General, and the latter instituted the Court Martial merely to divert the odium of misconduct from himself. Though the reputation of the Field Officer was at stake, the Court Martial never passed any Judgment, but the matter was hushed up; a certain proof that the Colonel was the victim of the General's power, who was himself chiefly

to

to blame for being absent, as has been stated, from his post.

When a circumstance like this is recited, every British Officer must feel a certain degree of self-congratulation. From the sense of Honour and Principles of Justice which pervade the Military Service of this Country, the lowest Subaltern has always a certain appeal against the tyranny of his Superior, however high may be his Rank. It may be in the judgment of a Commanding Officer to institute, or not, a Court-Martial; but when once instituted, no influence of his can direct, or avert its decision.

That 2,264 Men in a besieged Fortress, and drawn from a weak and sickly Garrison, should march out of the protection of their Works, to attack a Front of such Force and Extent, guarded by 410 men, and by Lines and Forts which covered them; and that they should succeed in carrying fire to the distance of 800 toises from the walls of the Garrison, in presence of an Army of 14,000 men, encamped at the small distance of a mile and a half from their Gates, is an Enterprize without example in the Annals of Military Service; and when it is considered that this sudden achievement was crowned with the most complete success, it is impossible to avoid fixing admiration on him who formed the Plan, as well as on those who had the honour of commanding and assisting in the execution of it.

It is known as a fact, by the acknowledgment of several Persons of Distinction in the Spanish Army, that the Construction and Materials of these Works, destroyed by the fire, cost the enormous sum of Thirteen Millions of

large

large Piastres, (equal to Three Millions Sterling) besides the considerable loss of Five Thousand Men, killed by the fire from the Garrison, and who died of distempers occasioned by excessive fatigue and unwholesome air, which prevailed in the Sands almost the whole year.

General ELIOTT's anxiety on the occasion would not permit him to await the issue in the Garrison, but as he had given the command of the Enterprize to Brigadier General Ross, he went out merely as a Volunteer. He probably considered it as his duty to be on the spot, lest any fatal accident should befall the Brigadier. Acquainting the Lieutenant-Governor therefore with his intention, he accompanied the *Sortie*. By the time the Advanced Corps had got possession of the Works, the General was in the front of the St. Carlos Battery, where he remained till the Retreat of the Detachment.

Brigadier Ross did not know of General ELIOTT's intention to go out, and as the latter followed the Detachment, the former was not acquainted with the circumstance till the Service was nearly performed. General Ross, with the utmost activity, had gone in person through the whole of the Enemy's Works, and after they had been carried, and the Troops had formed, upon his returning to take post in front of the 12th Regiment, General ELIOTT was pointed out to him, standing at the foot of the Battery. The General soon after accosted the Brigadier, who had expressed marks of surprize at seeing him, by asking him in an easy pleasant way, " What he " thought of the business, and if it was not something " extraordinary that they should have gained the Enemy's " Works so easily?" The Brigadier briskly replied to
the

the General, " That the most extraordinary thing was to see *him* there."

There was something noble in General ELIOTT's resolution to be present in the *Sortie*, and something equally so in his manner of doing it. As the Command had been publicly given to General ROSS, he would not hurt the feelings of that Officer, by going out at the head of the Detachment; he therefore contented himself with following it; and with a magnanimity worthy of him, he at all times imputed that merit to the Brigadier and his Detachment, which they so fully deserved, but a great share of which certainly attached to the Projector of the Enterprize.

While the Brigadier was in the Works to the Right, and after General ELIOTT had taken his station before the St. Carlos Battery, a Troop of Spanish Horse came out of the Lines, and galloped down in front of La MOTTE's and REDEN's Grenadiers, to reconnoitre the position of the British Troops, but made no attempt to outflank them. The Spanish Officer challenged the Hanoverians, and was answered by Colonel HUGO, " REDEN's Grenadiers;" while these veteran Soldiers stood with the utmost firmness and composure without charging or firing a single shot. Colonel HUGO immediately detached an Ordonnance to apprize the Brigadier of the appearance of this Troop of Horse. Sir JAMES FOULIS, the Town-Major, who, as one of General ELIOTT's Aides-du-Camp, had attended him out upon the Enterprize, received the intelligence, and conveyed it to the General, who instantly dispatched Sir JAMES with orders for the two Right-Hand Companies of the 12th and HAR-

L   DENBERG'S

DENBERG's, to wheel to the right, and form *en potence*, to be in readiness to oppose any force that might outflank the Parallel. This the General did in the absence of the Brigadier, and it was the only order which he gave during the whole of the Expedition.

The Troop of Horse attempted to go behind the second Line of Approach, with an intention further to reconnoitre; but coming up to the extremity of that Line, in the way to the Centre Barrier of the Lines, they found the fire from the high Batteries of the Rock, which had been ordered to range on that front with round-shot, and which was played very briskly, so fatal to them, that they were obliged to make the best of their way, in very great disorder, to the last Barrier on the East of their Lines.

In the spot where General ELIOTT stood, it was that the principal defence had been made, and after the Works had been carried, and while the Workmen were employed in firing them, his Humanity led him to see that all possible attention was paid to the wounded, whether of his own Troops or those of the Enemy. Amongst them, and almost expiring, he found an elegant young man, who was known by his Uniform to be a Captain of the Spanish Artillery. The General spoke to him with the tenderness which such a scene naturally inspires in a brave mind, and assuring him of all possible assistance, ordered him to be removed, as the fire was spreading rapidly to the spot where he lay. The Spaniard endeavoured to raise himself from the ground, and with the most expressive action, feebly articulated, " *No, Sir, no—leave me—Let me perish amidst the ruins of my post.*" An

Officer

Officer remained near him a few minutes, until he expired. It was afterwards found, that he had commanded the Guard of the St. Carlos Battery, and gallantly maintained his ground, until his Men, finding themselves overpowered, threw down their arms, and deserted him. He reproached their baseness, and exclaiming, " *at least one Spaniard shall die honourably*"—rushed down from the top of his Work amongst the attacking Column, and fell where he was found, at the foot, and in front of the Battery which he guarded. It was much lamented by General ELIOTT, and the Officers of the Detachment, that any doubt should have existed of the name of this gallant man; they believed it to have been Don JOSEPH BARBOZA; but there is still an uncertainty, which his Countrymen will, perhaps, one day feel it their duty to remove.

Two Spanish Officers, it has been observed, were carried prisoners into the Garrison. The one was Baron Von HELMSTADT, an Ensign in the Walloon Guards, with the rank of Captain; the other, Don VINCENTE FRIZA, a Lieutenant of Artillery.

Baron HELMSTADT having been severely wounded by a musquet shot in one of his knees, was found lying upon the platform of the St. Carlos Battery, by two British Artillery Soldiers, who, moved with generous compassion at his situation, resolved to rescue him from his impending fate. They took him up in their arms, and carried him out of the Battery, where he must soon have perished in the flames. Unwilling to leave him upon the sands in his helpless state, they determined upon carrying him into the Garrison. They were executing their noble purpose, when they met with Lieutenant CUPPAGE of their own

L 2   Corps,

Corps, who, while he bestowed the warmest encomiums
upon his men for their humanity, himself assisted in the
generous office which it suggested. With every possible
tenderness they conveyed the wounded Prisoner to the Barriers, where they did not arrive till two hours after the whole
Detachment had retired. During this time they had been
exposed to the fire of the Enemy's Lines, and had been
reported in the Garrison as lost. Having presented themselves at the Barrier, and being admitted, they passed
through the different Guards amidst the mingled admiration
and applause of the whole ; till they reached the Garrison
Hospital, where they deposited the Baron. On such an
instance of humanity, the mind dwells with an applauding
rapture. While strongly characteristic of the generous
disposition of a British Soldier towards a vanquished Enemy, it dignifies human nature, and illumines the rugged
front of war with the radiant emanations of Philanthropy.
To the feelings of a British Officer, any eulogium upon an
exercise of his humanity would wear the appearance of an
insult. Generosity to a conquered Enemy is a distinguishing
feature in the Military Character of this Country ; and it
seems indeed to be an axiom established by the stamp of
Omnipotence itself, that the most generous are invariably
the most brave. To the two Soldiers, the same considerations of delicacy do not so strongly apply as to their
Officer, and it becomes the peculiar duty of the Historian
to snatch from oblivion the names of two men, whose
feelings were equally an honour to their profession and their
species. They were named CAMPBELL and PATON, two
privates in the second Battalion of the Royal Regiment of
Artillery.

The wound in the Baron's knee was deemed incurable,
and it was not without great reluctance that he submitted

to

to an Amputation. When the Surgeons first informed him that an operation was absolutely indispensable, he resolutely opposed it. " Amputation," he said, " seldom succeeded in Spain ; besides, he was then betrothed in marriage to a Lady, and would rather risk his life than present himself before her with only one leg." The Governor being told of this determination, immediately visited the Baron, and used every argument to persuade him to comply. " His Mistress," the General kindly urged, "must undoubtedly esteem him the more for the honourable wound which he had received in the service of his Sovereign ; and as to the operation being fatal, he might almost assure himself of a certain recovery, since, in the many similar cases which had occurred in the Garrison during the Siege, the Surgeons had been generally successful ;"—and to convince him by ocular proof, several mutilated Convalescents were ordered into the room. This generous attention of the Governor had a powerful effect upon the Baron, and he at length consented to the operation. The day after it was performed, he was visited by the Governor, whom, upon entering his apartment, he addressed in these words— " *Ha! mon General! me voici un vieillard!*"

It must be satisfactory to pursue the account of this unfortunate young Officer without interruption. For many days after the Amputation, there was every prospect of his doing well; but, on the 28th of December, about a month after the operation had been performed, he died of an inflammatory fever. During his illness, Flags of Truce were daily passing and repassing, to inform his friends of his situation, who were not inattentive to him. They sent him fowls, and refreshments of different kinds, with a supply of money.

On

On the 29th, about noon, his body was conveyed from the Hospital to the New Mole, with every mark of Military Honour. The Grenadier Company of the 12th Regiment accompanied it, and the Governor, Major-General De la MOTTE, Captain CURTIS, and their Suites, with Don VINCENTE FRIZA, joined in the procession. As the Corpse was deposited in the boat, the 12th Grenadiers fired three Vollies over it, and the Town-Major and Secretary accompanied it. Sir Charles KNOWLES and the Adjutant-General preceded; in a Barge carrying a Flag of Truce, and delivered the Corpse to the Enemy, who in the same manner met them upon the occasion half-way over the Bay. Every thing sent by his friends, and left unused by the Baron in his sickness, was also returned, even to the minutest article.

Baron HELMSTADT had not been long in the Spanish Army, where he served as Ensign with the rank of Captain. The family of the Barons de HELMSTADT is of the Palatinate of the Rhine, where they have the following possessions, viz. the Estates of *Hockhausen*, and *Hardschuysheim*, near *Heidelberg*. The father of the Baron, whose melancholy but honourable end has just been recorded, was Chamberlain at the Court of the Elector-Palatine, and his Mother was the Baroness de KNOENING, in *Franconia*, and allied to the first families of that Province, and of the Lower Palatinate of the Rhine.

To return to the *Sortie*. Although the Attack was not totally exempted from those little derangements which generally attend Night Expeditions of this nature, yet, to the honour of the whole, neither musquet, working-tool, nor other implement was left behind. A Volunteer indeed of

the

the 73d Regiment lost his *kilt* in the Attack, which circumstance coming to the Governor's ear, he made a good jest of it upon the Parade, at the same time promising the Volunteer a warmer covering; and accordingly soon after he presented him with a Commission in a veteran Regiment.

The Public Orders on the morning after the *Sortie*, bore testimony to the sentiments of the General upon that great exploit. He expressed " that the bravery and con . duct of the whole Detachment, Officers, Sailors, and Soldiers, on the glorious occasion, surpassed his utmost acknowledgments."

During the following day, the Enemy's Works continued burning with great violence. In the course of the forenoon the Enemy fired a great many shells, and at night a very smart fire was kept up from the Garrison upon their Works, to prevent their extinguishing the fire.

About four o'clock in the morning of the 28th, the Enemy began to cannonade, and discharge a great many small arms at their Advanced Works, till a shell from the Garrison bursting in the St. Carlos Battery, their firing immediately ceased. It was conjectured that the Spaniards imagined that the Garrison were making a second Sally, either to destroy more of their Works, or carry off the Guns and Mortars. It was observed from several of the Batteries on the Rock, that just before the Enemy began to fire, an explosion took place in the St. Carlos Battery, like the bursting of a shell, in consequence of which their firing commenced. From the number of lights seen moving in the Enemy's Camp and round the Bay, it was concluded that their whole Camp was alarmed.

The

The Enemy in the last 24 hours fired 34 shot and 5 shells. At night their fire was brisker than on the preceding night, while from the Garrison it was likewise increased, to prevent them from extinguishing the flames in their Advanced Works, which continued burning very fiercely.

On the 29th, from the top of the Rock, five Mortars were to be seen dismounted in the St. Carlos Battery ; one Gun in the New Mortar Battery elevated at 45 degrees, and three in the Western Gun-Battery dismounted. The Enemy during this day fired several shells at the Upper Batteries, and into the Town.

On the 30th, the Enemy's Works were still burning in five different parts ; in the Western Gun-Battery, and in the large Traverse in the rear of it; the *Debouché* still on fire, and the new Line of Approach to the Mortar Battery.

The Enemy still continued their fire upon the Upper Batteries and the Town, the only revenge they could take for their recent loss and disgrace.

On the 1st of December, the Enemy's Works still smoaking in several places, and while a Flag of Truce was passing to the Garrison, they pulled from their Works several firebrands that had not yet taken fire, which occasioned a discharge upon them from the Rock.

On the 2d, the ruins of the Enemy's Works were still smoaking. They seemed to have been very completely destroyed, being apparently reduced to heaps of rubbish and sand.

The

The Patroles of the Enemy's horse were at this period very numerous during the night, perhaps from the apprehension of another *Sortie*; but these were generally annoyed with grape shot from the Rock.

No attempt had yet been made by the Spaniards to extinguish the fire in their Advanced Works. They contented themselves with venting their revenge by a brisk cannonade upon the Garrison, and by hanging in their Camp some of the unfortunate Soldiers who had been driven from their Works, and escaped into their Lines, on the night of the *Sortie*.

In the beginning of this month, however, they began to recover from the state of stupefaction into which they seemed to have been thrown by their recent misfortune and disgrace. Upwards of a thousand men were seen at work, making fascines, &c. for which purpose large quantities of brushwood were collected from the neighbouring country.

On the night of the 7th, they seemed determined to establish themselves at the Centre Stone Guard House, round which they made a Trench, and they at the same time lined with fascines part of the fourth branch of Approach. During these a very smart fire was directed towards them from the Garrison.

Their operations seemed now to be entirely defensive. The Western Stone Guard House on the side of the Bay, was unroofed in the same manner as the Centre Guard House, and strengthened with sand; with a Trench dug round at some distance in front. In these, strong Guards

M were

were nightly posted, to protect their remaining Works, which, on the 18th, still continued to smoke in several places.

By the close of this month the Enemy had made considerable progress in repairing their Works. They added to the Trench in front of the Centre Guard House, and repaired the fourth and fifth branches of Approach; and in the night of the 7th of January, they *debouched* from the fifth branch, and dug a Trench about fifteen or twenty yards long towards the East.

In the night of the 9th, they raised the Epaulement joining the Centre Guard House; and opened four embrasures, two on each side of the building. They were all masked with fascines, and appeared solely for Defence. During the night of the 12th they formed a Trench from the *Débouchure* of the fifth branch to the front of the ruins of the St. Carlos Battery, towards the Western Beach, part of which was lined with fascines. They also raised *Places d'Armes* on the flanks of the St. Carlos Battery.

In the night of the 17th, they raised a Work embracing each extremity of the fascine ditch in front of the Centre Redoubt, which rendered the post complete. On the morning of the 19th, four embrasures in this Redoubt were unmasked, and *animated* with four howitzers. The fire from the Garrison upon their working-parties was unremitting, and consequently, as before, their loss must have been very great. They erected, notwithstanding, a line of communication from the fourth branch to the Centre Redoubt.

On

On the night of the 23d, they repaired the Parapet of the St. Carlos Battery nine fascines in height, and began to rebuild the Magazine in the rear. Great quantities of fascines, chandeliers, &c. were in and about the Work. On the afternoon of the 24th, the Governor opened the Lower Batteries on this Work, which maintained a very brisk and well served discharge for several hours. The carcasses frequently set fire to the fascines, but the Enemy as frequently extinguished it.

In the night of the 30th, the Enemy were observed to be very busy to the eastward of the Centre Redoubt. The Batteries from the Rock instantly opened upon them, and drove them from the place. At day-break it was found they had traced out a Work of five sides, with a large opening in the rear; but this Work never was completed.

In the beginning of February the St. Carlos Battery appeared very nearly completed, consisting of an Epaulement with two shoulders: five dodging Traverses were erected in the rear, and behind them two larger ones for Magazines. The *Place d'Armes*, on each flank of the Battery, seemed finished. Part of the Parallel joining the fifth branch, in extent about forty yards, was likewise lined with fascines, and repaired.

In the night of the 2d, they restored the western part of the St. Martin's Battery, making only five embrasures to open upon the Town and Water-Port. The fire from the Garrison at this period was extremely brisk, and did the Enemy very considerable damage.

During the night of the 17th, a party of the Besiegers was discovered at the Eastern extremity of the Parallel.

In

In the morning it was discovered that they had traced out with fascines, a Work of five sides, leaving the gorge open at the West return from the Parallel, and which seemed to be for another Redoubt.

On the night of the 18th, they added five embrasures to the Gun-Battery, and left a space for two others; an addition which made it appear as if the whole was intended for one Battery, that before had been divided into two.

Their Traverses were occasionally set on fire by the British Artillery, but the Spaniards exerted themselves upon such occasions with great spirit and activity, though their losses from the fire of the Garrison must have been very considerable.

The progress of the Enemy in the restoration of their Batteries was slow, but they yet were constantly employed. Their Works, however, seemed rather for Defence than Attack, and every operation which they carried on appeared to have for its object, protection against another *Sortie*. Nothing could more strongly evince the impression which they had received of the spirit and exertion of the British Troops, afflicted as these really were by the Scurvy, and lightly as the Spaniards had thought of them before that memorable event, than that such an Army as that of the Besiegers should deem it necessary to direct their attention to defend themselves against the irruption of such inferior numbers, rather than to prosecute a vigorous Assault.

On the 8th of March Lieutenant CUPPAGE of the Royal Artillery was dangerously wounded, in the Royal
Battery,

Battery, by a splinter of a small shell, which burst immediately after being discharged from the Rock Gun.

In the end of this month the Garrison received a Reinforcement from England of the 97th Regiment, commanded by Colonel STAUNTON, but consisting entirely of unseasoned Recruits, who soon became sickly; many of them died, and the rest were of little service to the Garrison for a very considerable time.

On the 31st, in the evening, a shell set fire to the flank of the Eastern Redoubt, which the Spaniards termed the Mahon Battery, and the flame being assisted by a brisk discharge from the Garrison, it burned with great violence for several hours, before it was extinguished.

The Enemy had now raised the Communication to the Centre Redoubt, and erected several Traverses behind the fourth branch of Approach. They had likewise extended their Parallel in a continued direction with the old Work, for about 100 yards, with casks and fascines, banked up with sand.

In the beginning of April, the Camp of the Enemy was considerably enlarged, and several Corps were observed to be marching into it.

At this period the Governor ordered all the Northern Batteries to be furnished with grates, for heating shot; but no order was at the same time given for using them.

Several Gun-boats in frame had been sent from England in the *Vernon* Store-ship. These were put together, and

were

were found to carry an eighteen pounder with great conve-
nience, and consequently became of very considerable utility.

About this time it was that a new spirit seemed to have
been infused into the Spanish Camp. His CATHOLIC
MAJESTY, mortified at the disgrace that had been brought
upon his Arms, and the great loss he had sustained by the
Sortie in the month of November, publicly declared his
determination to have Gibraltar at all events, cost what it
would. It was now that they were to prepare for that
grand Attack by Sea and Land, which had so long been
projected ; and the ultimate success of which, the Spanish
Nation would not, for a moment, allow themselves to
doubt.

The Duke de CRILLON, to whom the Garrison of
Minorca had surrendered on the 15th of February preceding, was destined to take upon him the command of this
mighty Enterprize, and he was now preparing for the execution of it, flushed by recent Victory, and confident of
success. In the conquest of Minorca, however, there was
but little to boast of, as a Soldier could not reasonably
plume himself upon vanquishing an Hospital ; though the
brave men which it contained had, under the command of
General MURRAY, made a very spirited Defence. To the
Garrison of Fort St. Philip, consisting of considerably less
than a thousand sickly and decrepid Soldiers and Seamen,
pent up in confined and untenable Works, was opposed a
vigorous and well appointed Army of 14,000 men. Such
was the distressing appearance of the British Garrison,
when they marched out with the Honours of War, that
many of the Spanish and French Troops were said to have
shed tears of compassion as they passed them. Such at
least

least was the generous testimony of the Duc de CRILLON and Baron de FALKENHAYN, the French Commandant.

On such a Conquest, therefore, the Duke could not much pride himself, nor from thence anticipate the event of his vast projects against Gibraltar. This Conquest, however, unimportant as it was, seemed to re-animate the Spanish Camp, perhaps chiefly from the proof which it gave, that a British Garrison might at length be subdued by sickness and fatigue.

It was said that HIS CATHOLIC MAJESTY, in proof of his approbation of the conduct of the Duc de CRILLON, added to his other Titles that of *Duc de Mahon*; but that great General aimed at another still more flattering to his military pride: he hoped that the *Conquest of Gibraltar* would give him a claim to add the name of that Rock to his Titles; a Conquest which, as he had no doubt of achieving, he thought would rank him as the first General of his age. This ambition, though, as the event proved, extravagant, yet in a Soldier was laudable; and the Duc de CRILLON had proved himself to be not unworthy of general estimation. During the Siege at Minorca he had acted with spirit and judgment; and after the Surrender of the Garrison, he behaved with humanity and moderation.

On the 9th of April, a line of battle Ship, with seven large Vessels and Tartans, arrived in the Bay from the West, and anchored at Algeziras. A rumour of the intended Attack by Sea had reached the Garrison of Gibraltar, which induced the Governor and Chief Engineer to direct their attention principally to the Sea-line, and some little improvements in that quarter were consequently made.

On

On the 14th several of the large ships at Algeziras struck their yards and top-masts, and a great number of men appeared to be employed on board of them, circumstances which left the Garrison no room to doubt that they were intended to be fitted as Floating Batteries for the grand Attack. Parties of Workmen were constantly employed upon them, in opening port-holes, and covering their larboard sides with junk, which from its elasticity they no doubt imagined capable of resisting shot. The Enemy seemed likewise busily employed in landing Cannon and Military Stores beyond Point Mala. The buz of mighty preparation, in short, seemed to go through their whole Camp.

The Garrison were no longer doubtful of the intentions of the Spaniards. They saw that a vigorous Attack by Sea was meditated, and they calmly prepared for the event. At this time there were upwards of a hundred pieces of Cannon in the Artillery-Park of the Enemy.

On the 25th it was that the Engineers began to mine a Gallery from a place above Farringdon's Battery (*Willis's*) to communicate through the Rock to a notch or projection of the Rock, below Green's Lodge, in which the Governor purposed to construct a Battery.

In the end of May several Corsicans arrived at Gibraltar to offer their services to General ELIOTT, by whom they were very graciously received, and afterwards formed into an Independent Corps, the command of which was given to Signor LEONETTI, nephew to General PAOLI.

On the 26th of May, a large Fleet appeared from the East, upwards of a hundred sail of which in the evening entered

the

the Bay, and anchored between the River Palamones and Algeziras. Amongst these were three large Men of War, one of which had a flag at her mizen: the rest were vessels with Troops and Military Stores. On the three succeeding days they landed Twelve Battalions, making in all near Nine Thousand Men. As the Troops disembarked, they encamped in the rear of the second Line, extending towards *Buena Vista*, which had been fitted up for the Commander in Chief's Quarters.

On the 28th of this month, a Flag of Truce came from the Enemy, with a Letter from Mr. ANDERSON, a Merchant, who had left the Garrison a few days before, and was taken on his passage to Faro. Before the purport of the Flag was known, the Governor, speaking to the Officers near him, said, " he supposed the Duke had arrived, and now sent to summon the Garrison—his answer should be short—No, No ; and addressing himself to the Officers present, " he hoped the Gentlemen would all support him."

The exertions of the Enemy in their Camp, and amongst their shipping, were prodigious, and vessels of all kinds were daily arriving in the Bay, laden with materials for the Siege.

On HIS MAJESTY's Birth-Day, the last of the Garrison Gun-boats was launched. They were twelve in number, three carrying a 24 pounder each, and the rest eighteen pounders. They were manned from the *Brilliant* and *Porcupine* Frigates, and *Speedwell* Cutter, with twenty-one men each.

N   For

For some time past the Enemy had almost discontinued
their labours in their Advanced Works, and their fire upon
the Garrison was considerably slackened.   This interval
of tranquillity the Governor employed with indefatigable
zeal in repairing and improving the Works of the Garrison.

On the 11th of June, a shell from the Enemy fell through
the splinter-proof, at the door of the Magazine on Princess
Anne's Battery *(Willis's)*, and bursting, communicated
with the powder, which instantly blew up.   The explosion was so violent as to shake the whole Rock, and throw
the materials on both sides to an almost incredible distance
into the sea.   The Battery was very materially injured, and
fourteen Men were unfortunately killed, and fifteen wounded, by the accident.   Immediately after the report of the
explosion, and upon the appearance of the column of smoke,
the Enemy gave a loud huzza ; their drums beat to arms
in their Camp, and they kept up a brisk Cannonade upon
the spot where the accident happened for the remainder of
the day.

On the 14th a French Frigate, with eighteen or nineteen Polacres, &c. arrived in the Bay, from which was landed a body of French Troops; and on the 16th a new
Camp was observed between the Grand Magazine and the
Orange Grove.   On the succeeding day another French
Convoy of upwards of Sixty Sail, arrived from the Eastward, filled with French Troops, computed to amount to
Five Thousand Men.   On the 20th and 21st they disembarked, and encamped to the Eastward of the Stone Quarry,
immediately under the Queen of Spain's Chair.

Several

Several General Officers, both Spanish and French, about this time frequently visited the Lines, and some of them occasionally came out to view the Advanced Works. The Enemy's fire at this time was extremely inconsiderable, and on the evening of the 22d it totally ceased. At this period it was that the Duc de CRILLON arrived in Camp, to take upon him the command of the COMBINED ARMY.

From this period the Blockade was converted into a spirited Siege, and all those vast projects for the reduction of this Fortress, which had been so long agitated, were to be carried into vigorous effect.

The Duc de CRILLON was attended by Monsieur d'ARÇON, a French Engineer of reputation, who came to execute the Floating Batteries according to the Plan which he had given to the Spanish Court, and according to which they were to be constructed upon principles that were to render them *insubmersible* and incombustible.

This operation of the Attack by Sea had long been unanimously agreed upon, and no other question remained but respecting the means projected by M. d'ARÇON for executing it. His Plan was judged to be very simple, and was approved by all the Spanish Ministers; but he stated in the Memoir which he gave in with it, " that it would never succeed, unless a number of National Volunteers would adopt it, and execute it, at their own risk, with all the confidence inspired by a thorough conviction."

The Treasures of Spain, however, were to be lavished in these preparations, the impression of which, it was be-

N 2   lieved,

lieved, that Gibraltar could not resist for four and twenty hours. The most powerful means possible were to be put in practice, *pour coulbuter*, (according to the Spanish phrase) to overpower this Fortress. There certainly never was an instance of such a formidable force, and great preparations, as those of the Besiegers before Gibraltar. Almost all the Cannon and Howitzers upon the Isthmus battered the Place *d'enfilade*, and these, in the old and new Batteries of St. Philip and St. Barbara, with that of St. Barbe, and their several communications, amounted to the vast number of 246 pieces. Never was seen collected upon the same front, so vast a quantity of Ordnance, while in the Attack by Sea 213 other pieces of Artillery were to be employed, which were to take the Works of the Garrison in reverse, and by a *ricochetting* fire, increase the means of destruction. All their Batteries were to combine in the demolition of the Walls and Flanks, whilst the other part of their force was to be employed in ravaging the Interior Defences, in order to expose and sweep away the Soldiers of the Garrison.

General ELIOTT, with a firm and equal mind, beheld the operations of the Enemy. He felt all their strength; he anticipated every thing; and without giving the least ground of suspicion to the Besiegers, he made such preparations, and adopted such cautious measures, that the most dreadful display of force must have failed before them. He relied upon himself, he relied upon his Garrison, now inured to danger, to repel the most formidable Assault which human force and ingenuity could direct against him.

Rear

Rear Admiral BUENAVENTURA MORENO was appointed to co-operate with the Duke and M. d'ARÇON, in the projected Attack by Sea. The latter, however, now found himself, from the conduct of the Spanish Ministry, in such a situation, that although they allowed him certain discretionary powers, yet in case of success, all the Glory of the Enterprize was to be transferred to others, whilst the disgrace of a Miscarriage was to fall solely upon him, as the Projector of a Scheme which had not been crowned with success.

They proceeded, notwithstanding, with such expedition upon the Floating Batteries, that in the beginning of July, the tenth was under equipment. Since the arrival of the Duke, their Batteries had been wholly silent, notwithstanding which the Garrison kept up a brisk discharge, as well upon their Lines as their Advanced Works.

To detail all the preparatory operations of the Enemy, would far exceed the bounds of the present Work. It has already been observed, that the preparations made for the Attack by Sea were formidable and immense, and the consequent expence incurred by Spain has scarcely a parallel in History. The activity of the Enemy was proportioned to the magnitude of the design, and the Attack by Land, as an auxiliary operation, was to occupy all the space that the nature of the ground would permit.

The morning of the arrival of Mons. le Comte d'ARTOIS, which happened on the 15th of August, was distinguished by the complete developement of a *flying sap* of a new kind, the erection of which had been concealed from the Garrison by a silence and rapidity of execution as yet unequalled. This was a Parallel of 230 toises in length, with a Communication or *Boyau* of 630 toises from the place where it was joined to the principal Barrier of the Lines, the construction of which had required *one million six hundred thousand* bags of sand, besides an immense quantity of casks employed in the Parallel, which was afterwards converted into a Battery of 64 Cannons, besides howitzers, at the extremity, to the South East, and four Batteries of Mortars to the North West.

In one night was this extraordinary Work of the *Epaulement* raised to the incredible height of 12 feet, with a proportional thickness of 18 feet. With its Communications, Traverses, and Branches, it formed a prospect equally formidable and surprising. It was calculated, that during the seven hours in which this Work was erected, ten thousand men must have been employed upon it. Notwithstanding this immense number at work at one time, no extraordinary noise was heard. In the course of the night a Carcass was thrown on the West side of the Bay, but, nothing of their operations was to be seen in that quarter. The Spaniards must have conceived themselves particularly fortunate, as a brisk fire from the Garrison, from the number of men employed in their Works, must have proved more than commonly destructive.

General ELIOTT, and General GREEN, the Chief Engineer of the Garrison, instantly discovered the design of the Enemy by this extension of their Works, which was to take in reverse the Defences to the Sea, in order to co-operate with the Floating Batteries and Bomb-Ketches, and thus to place the Artillery of the Garrison between two fires, when the Grand Attack should be made.

On

On the 16th the Duc de BOURBON arrived in the Enemy's Camp; and on the 19th General ELIOTT received by a Flag of Truce, the following Letter from the Duc de CRILLON.

" *Camp of Buena-Vista,* 19th *August,* 1782.

" SIR,

" His Royal Highness Count d'Artois, who has received
" permission from the King his Brother to assist at the
" Siege, as a Volunteer in the Combined Army, of which
" their Most Christian and Catholic Majesties have honour
" ed me with the command, arrived in this Camp the 15th
" instant. This young Prince has been pleased, in passing
" through Madrid, to take Charge of some Letters which
" had been sent to that Capital from this place, and which
" are addressed to persons belonging to your Garrison.
" His Royal Highness has desired that I would transmit
" them to you, and that to this mark of his goodness and
" attention, I should add the strongest Expressions of
" Esteem for your Person and Character. I feel the great-
" est pleasure in giving this mark of condescension in this
" august Prince, as it furnishes me with a pretext, which I
" have been anxiously looking for these two months that I
" have been in Camp, to assure you of the highest Esteem
" I have conceived for your Excellency, of the sincerest de-
" sire I feel of deserving yours, and of the pleasure to
" which I look forward of becoming your Friend, after I
" shall have learned to render myself worthy of the honour,
" by facing you as an Enemy. His Highness the Duc de
" Bourbon, who arrived here twenty-four hours after the
" Count d'Artois, desires also that I should assure you of
" his particular Esteem.

" Permit me, Sir, to offer a few trifles for your table, of
" which I am sure you must stand in need, as I know you
" live

" live entirely upon Vegetables: I should be glad to know
" what kind you like best. I shall add a few Game for the
" Gentlemen of your Household, and some Ice, which I
" presume will not be disagreeable in the excessive heat of
" this climate, at this season of the year. I hope you will be
" obliging enough to accept the small portion which I send
" with this Letter.

" I have the honour to be, &c.

" B. B. Duc de CRILLON.

" *His Excellency General Eliott, &c."*

On the 20th, the General returned by a Flag the following Answer.

" *Gibraltar, August 20th,* 1782.

" Sir,

" I find myself highly honoured by your obliging Letter
" of yesterday, in which your Excellency was so kind as to in-
" form me of the arrival in your Camp, of his Royal High-
" ness the Count d'Artois, and the Duke de Bourbon, to
" serve as Volunteers at the Siege. These Princes have
" shewn their judgement in making choice of a Master in
" the Art of War, whose Abilities cannot fail to form great
" Warriors. I am overpowered with the condescension of
" his Royal Highness, in suffering some Letters for persons
" in this Town to be conveyed from Madrid in his Carri-
" ages. I flatter myself that your Excellency will give my
" most profound Respect to his Royal Highness, and to the
" Duke de Bourbon, for the Expressions of Esteem with
" which they have been pleased to honour so insignificant
" a person as I am.

" I return a thousand Thanks to your Excellency for
" your handsome Present of Fruits, Vegetables, and Game.
" You will excuse me, however, I trust, when I assure
" you,

" that in accepting your Present, I have broken through a
" resolution to which I had faithfully adhered since the be-
" ginning of the War; and that was, never to receive or .
" procure, by any means whatever, any provisions or other
" commodity for my own private use: so that, without any
" preference, every thing is sold publicly here; and the
" private Soldier, if he has money, can become a purchaser,
" as well as the Governor.   I confess, I make it a point of
" honour to partake both of plenty and scarcity in common
" with the lowest of my brave Fellow Soldiers.   This fur-
" nishes me with an excuse for the liberty I now take, of
" intreating your Excellency not to heap any more Favours
" upon me of this kind, as in future I cannot convert your
" Presents to my own private use.   Indeed, to be plain with
" your Excellency, though Vegetables at this season are
" scarce with us, every man has got a quantity proportioned
" to the labour which he has bestowed in raising them.
" The English are naturally fond of gardening and cultiva-
" tion; and here we find our amusement in it, during the
" intervals of rest from public duty.   The promise which
" the Duke de Crillon makes, of honouring me in proper
" time and place with his Friendship, lays me under infinite
" obligations.   The interest of our Sovereigns being once
" solidly settled, I shall with eagerness embrace the first
" opportunity to avail myself of so precious a treasure.

" I have the honour to be, &c.

" G. A. ELIOTT.

" *His Excellency the Duc de Crillon, &c.*"

On the morning of the 24th, their new Work was completed, and unmasked a Battery of 64 guns, with 8 howitzers on its left extremity.   The plan of operations pursued
by the Enemy now became apparent to the General, who
continued to make every arrangement to defeat it, and who

O   now

now digested the plan of disposition, in case they should effect a practicable Breach. At this period additional forges for heating shot were ordered to be constructed, and grates for that purpose were distributed all along the Batteries.

In the Spanish Camp, the successful execution of the Sap on the night of the 15th, was looked upon as a fortunate and auspicious event, though the plan of this operation, which had been suggested by M. d'Arçon, had not met with very general approbation, from the great apprehension that was entertained of a considerable loss of men in carrying it into effect.

The Land and Sea Forces of the Besiegers flattered themselves with the hope, that in these preparations, the term of their long and glorious labours was drawing to a close; and the solidity and equipment of their new warlike machines, inspired them with a degree of confidence, which soon increased to enthusiasm. This spirit produced a competition amongst the Officers, who emulously aspired to the honour of conducting these formidable engines in the presence of their Enemy. The Combined Army, in short, flattered themselves that nothing was wanting to their success. They had only, they imagined, to present themselves—Gibraltar was to be taken in twenty-four hours—and thus their confidence approached to infatuation.

From the time of the Duc de CRILLON's arrival before Gibraltar, however, a disposition had been made, and was given in the Standing Orders of the Field, in order to prevent a *Sortie* from the Fortress, which, notwithstanding

standing its small Garrison, the Enemy still dreaded, after the disaster which had befallen them on the night of the 27th of November, 1781. This disposition of the Besiegers consisted of a Reserve of Infantry and Dragoons, who held themselves always in readiness to act during the night. This Body of Reserve was posted upon the Isthmus behind the Lines, or upon the right of the Escarpments of the Mountain, next the Mediterranean, and behind the Parallel, or Boyau, according to the discretion of the Brigadier who had the command for the night. It was ordered, that in case the Garrison should attempt a *Sortie*, he should make a brisk march with his Right Flank towards the North Escarpments, and boldly take post before the Pallisade at the head of the Moat. As in that situation, the fire of the Garrison would be necessarily suspended upon that spot, for fear of hurting their own men, the Spaniards would risk but little by the manœuvre.

In the beginning of September the Enemy's Works on the land side were every hour advancing to perfection ; but the Duc de CRILLON's attention towards completing them seemed so entirely to engage him, as in a great measure to prevent his taking the necessary precautions for their defence against the Batteries of the Rock. He seemed to conclude, that the Garrison, awed by his mighty preparations, would not be in a condition for any offensive attempt ; and relying upon this belief, or never taking it into the account at all, the Advanced Batteries in the Parallel, as well as those in the Lines, undergoing alterations and repair, were wholly stript of their Ordnance. The Forts, and a few Mortar Batteries, were of course the only defences left to protect these immense Works from insult and attack.

O 2   The

The practicability of an attempt upon them in this state, strongly suggested itself to Lieutenant-General BOYD, the Lieutenant-Governor, and the honour of the consequent success was peculiarly his own. On the morning of the 6th of September, he recommended, by Letter to the Governor, the immediate use of red-hot shot against the Land Batteries of the Besiegers. General ELIOTT readily assented, and Major LEWIS, the Commandant of Artillery, was ordered to wait on General BOYD for his instructions. By the morning of the 8th every thing was ready. At seven in the morning of that day, the firing commenced from all the Northern Batteries which bore upon the Parallel, and was supported through the day with admirable vivacity. The effect of the red-hot shot exceeded expectation. In two hours, the Mahon Battery of six guns, with the Battery of two howitzers on its Flank, and great part of the adjoining Parallel, were on fire; and the flames, notwithstanding the Enemy's exertions to extinguish them, burnt with such rapidity, that the whole of those Works were consumed before night. The St. Martin's Battery was frequently on fire, but which was as frequently extinguished; and though that of St. Carlos escaped the flames, yet they were both so much deranged by the breaches made to obstruct the effects of the carcasses, &c. that the greater part of them were obliged to be taken down.

The Enemy did not return the fire till eight o'clock, and that but faintly, from the Seven Gun Battery in the Lines only. About half past nine St. Philip and St. Barbara, and soon after, eight new Mortar Batteries in the Parallel, were opened upon the Garrison. Their tardiness in returning the fire, it was conjectured, was owing to the

con-

confused state of their Batteries, from the repairs they were undergoing, or to their wanting particular orders how to act, as a General Officer was seen to enter their Lines at the time the Cannonade became general. Their Batteries at the time too were unprovided with Ammunition, and the discharge of red-hot shot rendered it particularly dangerous to carry it down from the Lines.

The loss of the Enemy in sight of the Garrison, was very great, as their endeavours to stop the progress of the flames very much exposed them to the fire from the Rock. The success of this day was attended with the happiest effects, as it provoked the Enemy to open their new Mortar Batteries before they were perfectly completed, and to recommence a fire from their Forts and Lines, for which they were by no means prepared.

About four o'clock in the afternoon the firing abated on both sides, and by night-fall it had totally ceased. This judicious plan of Attack, suggested by the Lieutenant-Governor, produced very signal advantages. It in a great measure, by precipitating them, deranged the operations of the Duc de CRILLON; and it convinced the Enemy that the Garrison, unawed by their formidable preparations, were still in a state for offensive measures.

The Duke, however, seemed resolved to retaliate, for on the succeeding morning, at half-past five o'clock, upon two rockets being thrown up from Forts St. Philip and Barbara, the Enemy began with a flight of shells from all the Advanced Batteries, to bombard and cannonade the Garrison. About a hundred and seventy pieces of Ordnance were open; but the effect was not proportionate, for though at times, from

from ten to twenty shells were in the air at the same moment, they happily did not produce that material damage
which there was reason to expect.

On the same day the Enemy's Squadron, consisting of
seven sail of the line, Spanish, and two French, with a
large frigate and xebec, taking the advantage of a Levant
wind, got under sail from the Orange Grove, and one of
them passing slowly within random shot, fired several
broadsides upon the South Bastion and Ragged Staff, con-
tinuing the Cannonade until she had got beyond Europa.
The Squadron then stood to the Eastward of the Rock,
and forming in a Line, the Admiral leading, came before
the Batteries of Europa, and under a very slow sail commenced a fire from all their Guns, until the last ship
had passed. They repeated this manœuvre at two o'clock
on the following morning, and again in the forenoon of the
same day. By this Sea-Attack, however, the Works of
the Garrison were not at all affected. Some of the leading
ships came pretty near the point of the first Attack; but
having been frequently struck from the English Batteries,
they afterwards kept at a greater distance. Two of the
Spanish ships went early that morning to Algeziras to
repair. All the Batteries at Europa were manned by the
Marine Brigade encamped there, with a small proportion
of Artillerists. The Guns were extremely well laid and
pointed; the whole under the immediate command of
Brigadier Curtis.

About five in the afternoon of the same day, sixteen of
the Enemy's Gun-boats went over from Algeziras, formed
in a line, and fired upon the Garrison; but in less than an
hour

hour were obliged to retire, with very considerable damage.

It was generally believed that this united Attack by Sea and Land was part of the plan of M. d'ARçON, by which the Garrison were to be placed between two fires, and thus severely harrassed and distressed. The Attack by Sea, however, of this day, was merely a spectacle furnished by the Duc de CRILLON to the French Princes, who went to *Buena Vista*, the Head Quarters of the Duke, in order to view it. They had never seen a Sea Attack, and the natural politeness of the Duke readily led him to gratify them. Though both extremities of the Rock were rendered very warm by the fire of the Enemy, yet the loss sustained by the Garrison was comparatively small, and the Works were very little injured. On the other hand, the ships of the Enemy were considerably damaged, and their losses in the Advanced Works must have been great.

Their Floating Batteries, to the number of Ten, were now completed, and M. d'ARçON, notwithstanding the cause of dissatisfaction which he felt, had been zealous in superintending their equipment. When he delivered his opinion, in a Council of War, upon the means of Attack, the point was, he urged, to avoid an unfortunate disposition, by an extended Line of Attack which would be weak throughout the whole. The Commander in Chief replied to him, " you have the affection of a Parent for your Batteries—you think of nothing but preserving them." This occurred before they were completed, but M. d'ARçON still continued to assist in the Council, and endeavoured to speak his sentiments there freely. Upon one of
these

these occasions the Duc de CRILLON said to him, in the presence of M. le Comte d'ARTOIS, " When I asked " that they should send for you into Spain, (for it was I " who requested that you should come) it was for the pur- " pose of executing my Plan for the Attack of Gibraltar " with Floating Batteries. Now, Sir, your Commission " is fulfilled: the rest belongs to me."

When the Battery *Paula Prima* was proved for the Attack, it was perceived that there was a deficiency of Water for preventing the effect of the red-hot balls. The General and all the Commanding Officers were informed of this defect; but they thought so lightly of it, that Don CAYETAN LANGARA pleasantly said, " he would under- take to receive on his breast all the red-hot balls of the Enemy." Notwithstanding the pressing entreaties of M. d'ARÇON, that an essay should be made with red-hot balls upon this Battery, before opening it against the Garrison, as he apprehended that the want of a constant circulation of water round the top would be found a very material defect, his request of an experiment was refused. The truth was, that the English Fleet, which was to bring relief to the Besieged, was at Sea; the season was far advanced, and no other course could be taken but to hasten the Attack from these Batteries before its arrival. Things being so situated, it was not probable that the Enemy would sus- pend their operations on account of the red-hot balls, which they generally despised.

On the 10th, at morning gun fire, the discharge from the Batteries on the Isthmus recommenced. At seven o'clock on that morning, including the expenditure of the 8th, they had discharged 5427 shot, and 2502 shells, ex-

clusive

clusive of the fire from the Men of War and Mortar Boats.

At Guard Mounting on the succeeding morning, they recommenced their cannonade, and in the afternoon of that day Detachments of Soldiers were seen embarking from the Enemy's Camp on board their Battering Ships. From this it was concluded in the Garrison that every thing was ready, and the Grand Attack about to commence. Land-Port and Water-Port Guards were therefore immediately reinforced; the furnaces and grates for heating shot were lighted, and the Batteries ordered to be manned.

While the attention of the Garrison was chiefly directed to the sea line, the Enemy, immediately after night-fall, attempted to set fire to the Pallisades at Bay-side and Forbes's, and in some measure succeeded, as the whole were quickly in flames. The Northern Guards and Piquets were immediately under arms, and a smart discharge of musquetry was directed upon several parties, which by the light of the fire were discovered in the meadows. These Parties returned a brisk discharge by platoons upon the Queen's Lines, while a greater number of shells than usual were thrown from the Enemy's Works. Their fire in the last twenty-four hours amounted to 2828 shot, and 1450 shells. On the morning of the 12th, at a quarter past one, when the Garrison had scarcely recovered from the alarm on the land-side, the Enemy's Gun and Mortar Boats appeared off the King's Bastion, and Old Mole Head, and began a very warm cannonade on the Northern Front. As they kept at a considerable distance, the

P   Garrison

Garrison returned their fire very sparingly, and they at length retired.

At seven A. M. a Fleet appeared from the Westward, and stood in for the Bay. It proved to be the Combined Fleets of France and Spain, consisting of thirty-eight large Ships of the Line, besides a great number of smaller vessels. No less than ten Admiral's Flags and a Broad Pendant were displayed on board of them. By the afternoon they were all at anchor between the Orange Grove and Algeziras.

The whole force of the Allied Crowns seemed to have been concentrated in this spot, and such a Naval and Military Spectacle is scarcely to be equalled in the Annals of War. Their Naval Force consisted of Forty-four large Ships of the Line, besides three inferior two-deckers, ten Battering Ships, five Bomb-Ketches, several Frigates and Xebecs, a great number of Gun and Mortar Boats, a large Floating Battery, many Armed Vessels, and near Three Hundred Boats purposely constructed for carrying Troops.

The Land Batteries, as has been stated, were furnished with two hundred and forty-six pieces of Cannon, Mortars and Howitzers; and the Combined Army now amounted to Forty Thousand, while the numbers of the Garrison at this period, fit for duty, exceeded, by a very few only, Seven Thousand Men.

The immense forces of the Enemy were besides animated by the immediate presence of two Princes of the
Royal

Royal Blood of France, and many of the Nobility of Spain; and the confidence inspired by their formidable preparations left no doubt of success. The Garrison, on the other hand, had nothing to rely upon but their own conduct and courage. Their confidence was not inspired by their numbers, but the tried ability of their Commanders, and the invincible bravery of the Men. They saw the prodigious force which was to be concentrated against them, but they firmly felt themselves equal to the encounter. They besides anticipated, in the defeat of that mighty force, a respite from the arduous though glorious labours in which they had been so unremittingly engaged.

It had been determined on the 4th of September, in a Council of War held in the Spanish Camp, that the Attack should be made between the Old Mole and the King's Bastion. The Commander in Chief ordered the Attack by a Letter addressed to the Commander of the Floating Batteries, the Admiral BUENAVENTURA MORENO.

On the 13th of September, at eight in the morning, all the Battering Ships were put in motion, and advanced to the several stations it had been previously determined they should occupy. They were ten in number.

Names of the Battering Ships.	Guns in use.	Guns in reserve.	Men.	Commanders.
Pastora	21	10	760	Rear Admiral Buenaventura Moreno.
Tallia Piedra	21	10	760	Prince of Nassau.
Paula Prima	21	10	760	Don Cayetan Langara.
El Rosario	19	10	700	Don Francisco Xafier Munos.
St. Christoval	18	10	650	Don Frederico Gravino.
Principe Carlos ...	11	4	400	Don Antonio Basurta.
San Juan	9	4	340	Don Joseph Angeler.
Paula Secunda ...	9	4	340	Don Pablo de Cosa.
Santa Anna	7	4	300	Don Joseph Goicochea.
Los Dolores	6	4	250	Don Pedro Sanchez.
	142	70	5260	

About thirty-six Men to each Gun in use, besides Sailors, &c. to work the Ships.

The *Pastora* and the *Tallia Piedra* were the first that received the fire from the Fortress. The others did not cast anchor till some time afterwards. The Admiral placed himself upon the Capital of the King's Bastion; the other ships extending, three to the Southward of the Flag, as far as the Church Battery; five to the North-ward, about the height of the Old Mole; and one a little to the Westward of the Admiral. Twenty-four Bomb-Ketches also acted in the wings, in the rear of the Attack. M. d'ARÇON served as a Volunteer in the Battery *Tallia Piedra*. By a quarter before ten they had taken their respective stations, at the distance of a thou-sand or twelve hundred yards, when a heavy cannonade commenced from all the Ships, supported by the Cannon and Mortars in the Enemy's Lines and Approaches, the object of which clearly was, not to leave the Garrison a single point of safety in the space behind the front at-tacked by the Floating Batteries. The Garrison Batteries were opened with hot and cold shot from the Guns, and shells from the Howitzers and Mortars. This firing conti-nued on both sides, without intermission, till noon, when that of the Enemy from their ships seemed in a small degree to slacken. About two o'clock the Admiral's Ship was observed to smoke, as if on fire; and a few men seemed busy upon the roof searching for the cause. The fire from the Garrison Batteries continued powerful and well-directed, while that from the Enemy's Ships gradually decreased. About seven in the Evening they fired from a few Guns, and that only at intervals. At midnight the Admiral's Ship was plainly discovered to be on fire, and an hour after, the flames burst forth with unconquerable violence. Eight more of the ships took fire in succession. On the preceding evening, when their fire began to slacken,

various

various signals had been made from the southernmost ships, and as the evening advanced, many rockets were thrown up, to inform their friends of their extreme danger and distress. These signals were immediately answered, and the launches, feluccas, and boats of the whole fleet, began to take out the men from on board the burning ships. Many shot were still fired from those in which the flames had yet made no considerable progress; and the fire from the Enemy's Batteries on shore did not in the least abate. Brigadier CURTIS, who, with his squadron of Gun-boats, lay ready to take advantage of any favourable circumstance, left the New Mole at two o'clock in the morning, and about three formed a line upon the Enemy's flank, advancing and firing with great order and expedition; which so astonished and disconcerted the Enemy, that they fled precipitately with all their boats, abandoning the ships, in which some Officers and numbers of their men, including many wounded, were left to perish. This must inevitably have been their wretched fate, had they not been dragged from amidst the flames, by the personal intrepidity of Brigadier CURTIS, at the utmost hazard of his own life, a life pronounced by General ELIOTT, to be invaluable to HIS MAJESTY's Service. Whilst the Brigadier, with his men, was thus generously employed, the flames reached the Magazine of one of the Battering Ships to the Northward, which blew up about five o'clock, with a dreadful explosion. In a quarter of an hour after, another, in the Centre of the Line, met with a similar fate, the wreck from which spread to a vast extent, and involved the Gun-boats in the most imminent danger. One of them was sunk by it, and the boat of Brigadier CURTIS had a hole made in its bottom, by a large splinter; the

Coxswain

Coxswain at the same instant was killed, and some others of the men wounded, and they were for a considerable time involved in a thick cloud of smoke. The Brigadier's barge was only saved from sinking by stopping the hole with the Seamen's jackets, until boats arrived to their relief. After this very fortunate escape, it was deemed prudent to withdraw towards the Garrison, to avoid the peril threatened by the blowing up of the remaining ships. The Brigadier, however, visited two other ships on his return, and landed nine Officers, two Priests, and three hundred and thirty-four private Soldiers and Seamen, all Spaniards, which, with one Spanish Officer, and eleven Frenchmen, who had floated on shore upon a piece of wreck on the preceding evening, made the total number saved amount to three hundred and fifty-seven. Many of the Prisoners were severely, and some of them dreadfully wounded. They were conveyed to the Hospital, where every attention was paid them which Humanity could dictate.

In the course of the day, the remaining eight ships severally blew up with violent explosions; one only escaped the effect of the red-hot shot, which it was thought proper to burn, there being no possibility of saving her. The Admiral's Flag remained flying on board his ship till she was totally consumed.

The Royal Artillery, additional Gunners, and Marine Brigade, were chiefly employed in the important service of the day, which they executed with a degree of activity, coolness, bravery, and effect, beyond the reach of adequate panegyric. The fire was incessant, and the Batteries abundantly supplied with Ammunition, every Sol-

dier

dier in the Garrison, not on duty, eagerly pressing to
share in the honourable labours of the day.

The Governor took his station on the King's Bastion,
the point of Attack of the Spanish Admiral and his Se-
conds; and Lieutenant-General Boyd posted himself on
the South Bastion, both animating by their presence the
great exertions of the men. The Besiegers had considerably upwards of Four Hundred Pieces of Ordnance in
play upon the Garrison, while only eighty Cannon, seven
Mortars, and nine Howitzers, were brought in use by
the latter.

The Enemy's Camp was filled, and the neighbouring
hills covered with an astonishing concourse of Spectators,
assembled to view, as they imagined, the reduction of the
British Fortress; for from the magnitude of the preparations, the Spanish Nation would never for a moment
allow themselves to doubt of the event.

By the information of the Prisoners it was learnt, that
their principal objects in this Attack were the King's
Bastion, and Line-Wall, north of Orange's Bastion.
Their largest ships were stationed off the former, in order
to silence that important Battery, whilst a breach was
attempted by the rest, in the curtain extending from the
latter to Montague's Bastion. If a breach had been effected, the Grenadiers of their Army were to have stormed
the Garrison under cover of the Combined Fleets. The
private men complained bitterly of their Officers, for
having represented the Battering-Ships as invulnerable,
and for having deceived them by a promise of their being
supported by Ten Sail of the Line, and all the Gun and

Mortar

Mortar Boats. They had been led to believe, that the Garrison could not fire many rounds of red-hot balls, but their consternation was indescribable, when they discovered that these were fired with the same precision and vivacity as cold shot.

Admiral MORENO had quitted the *Pastora*, his Flag Ship, a little before midnight, but some others of the Officers had retired much earlier. The loss sustained by the Enemy could never be properly ascertained; but from the information of the Prisoners, and the numbers seen dead on board the ships, it was estimated at Two Thousand Men, including the Prisoners.

The loss of the Garrison, on the other hand, when the duration and quantity of the Enemy's fire are considered, was almost incredibly trifling. It consisted in one Officer, and fifteen Men Killed; five Officers, and sixty-three Men Wounded. The Officer killed was Captain REEVES, of the Royal Artillery: those wounded, Captains GROVES and SIWARD, with Lieutenant GODFREY of that Corps; Lieutenant WETHAM of the 58th Regiment; and Captain MACKENZIE of the 73d.

The damage done to the Works bore no proportion to the violence of the Attack, and the excessive Cannonade which had been directed against them. The Merlons of the different Batteries were disordered, and the flank of Orange's Bastion was a little injured. The latter was chiefly done by the land-fire, but was not of such consequence as to afford any ground for apprehension. The Ordnance and Carriages were also damaged; but by the

Q   activity

activity of the Artillery, the whole Sea-line, before night, was in serviceable order.

On the succeeding day a Flag of Truce went with a Letter from General ELIOTT to the Duc de CRILLON, and some Letters from the Spanish Officers, Prisoners, were sent by the same conveyance. The gratitude expressed by all the Prisoners, for their deliverance from the complicated horrors with which they were surrounded, was gratifying to Humanity. They had been led to expect no quarter from the British Garrison, an opinion artfully instilled by their Officers, to aid their courage by the suggestions of despair.

On the following day the Duc de CRILLON returned an answer by a Flag, to the Governor's Letter of the preceding day.

On the 17th the Seamen raised the Gun-boat that had been sunk by the blowing up of one of the Battering Ships. In the evening of the same day, all the Spanish Officers were sent by a Flag of Truce to their Camp.

The Enemy had continued their fire from their Lines and Advanced Works, with little intermission, which was briskly returned from the Northern Batteries of the Rock. Their Fleet had lain inactive since the fate of the Floating Batteries; but on the 20th their Mortar Boats bombarded the Garrison, though at a very respectful distance.

From this period the fire of the Enemy seemed to be under a certain regulation. About five or six in the

morning

morning their Cannonade commenced, which was continued very briskly till noon. From twelve to two o'clock
they generally intermitted, for the purpose of taking their
siesta, or mid-day nap, and in the decline of day, they
fired more or less as their caprice directed. About seven
in the evening the Cannon ceased, and their Mortars
took up the fire, which they generally continued till day-
break of the succeeding morning. The Ammunition
expended was generally from four to five, and sometimes
six hundred shells, in the twenty-four hours, with from
six hundred to a thousand shot.

After the signal failure of their great attempt, the Spaniards probably gave up the hope of reducing Gibraltar
by force, but they evidently relinquished that hope with
great reluctance, for the Combined Fleets still remained
in the Bay, with a view to oppose the Relief of the Garrison, which was about this time to be attempted by Lord
HOWE.

On the 4th of October, Captain CURTIS went in his
Barge to the Orange Grove, from whence he was conducted in a Carriage to Buena Vista, the General's Head
Quarters, for the purpose of establishing a Cartel with
the Enemy for the exchange of Prisoners. He was introduced by the Duc de CRILLON to His Royal Highness
the Count d'ARTOIS, who thanked him, in very handsome terms, for his humanity and gallantry in relieving
the unfortunate Prisoners from the burning Battering Ships:
he at the same time requested him to convey to the Governor his warmest acknowledgments for his benevolence
and liberality upon the same unhappy occasion. In the

evening

evening Captain CURTIS returned to the Garrison in the same manner in which he had gone.

On the 4th, two of the Enemy's Engineers had been observed picketing out a Work, extending from the ruins of the Mahon Battery to the Western Beach, crossing the North West Angle of the farther Gardens. During the night of the 5th, they erected a strong Boyau of Approach, extending in the line before-mentioned, about four hundred and thirty yards. It was raised with sandbags, and was conjectured by the British Engineers to be a Communication to some additional Works projected by the Enemy. At night the Old Mole head Howitzers and the Upper Batteries, opened upon this Work, and as the former almost entirely *enfiladed* it, the Enemy were so much annoyed, that they could not complete it. On the succeeding night, however, they finished the Communication to the Parallel, from the extremity of the Boyau, near the ruins of the Mahon Battery, which had been left imperfect on the preceding night. From these operations of the Enemy it appeared that they had not relinquished the Siege, but on the contrary, seemed inclined to prosecute it, hopeless as they were of success, with an increased activity and vigour.

The Combined Fleets had been reinforced, by the occasional arrival of Ships, both of the Line and inferior rates. On the evening of the 10th, a very fresh westerly wind set in, which, as the night advanced, increased to a hurricane. In the course of the night many signal-guns of distress were fired from the Ships of the Combined Fleet, and at day-break the St. Michael, a Spanish ship, mounting seventy-two guns, was discovered in a crippled state,

state, close in-shore, off Orange's Bastion: she was under close reefed courses, and had lost her mizen-top-mast. After having two men killed and two wounded by the Garrison-Batteries, she fell on shore near to the South Bastion, and immediately struck her Colours. She was soon afterwards taken possession of by Captain CURTIS, who expeditiously landed the prisoners, and carried out anchors to prevent her going further on shore. She was commanded by DON JUAN MORENO, a Chief d'Escadre, and had on board about six hundred and fifty men. She was afterwards got off without having sustained any damage, and was condemned as a lawful prize to the Garrison of Gibraltar. The Fleet of the Enemy had suffered very much by the gale; a Ship of the Line and a Frigate were on shore near the Orange Grove, and a French Ship of the Line had lost her fore-mast and bowsprit. Two others were forced from their anchors, and ran to the Eastward.

At three in the afternoon of the 11th, the signals made by the Enemy indicated the approach of the British Fleet. About sun-set of that day, the *Latona* Frigate anchored under the Walls of the Garrison, at which time the Van of the British Fleet was perceived in the Gut. The Spanish Admiral shewed no disposition to oppose the Reinforcements being thrown into the Garrison, but from a want of timely attention to the circumstances of the Navigation, only four or five Transports could enter the Bay. The rest, with the Fleet, were obliged to pass to the Eastward into the Mediterranean. The Fleet consisted of Thirty-four Sail of the Line, Eleven of which were three-deckers, with six Frigates, and thirty-one Ordnance Transports, conveying a reinforcement of upwards of sixteen hundred men for the Garrison.

Early

Early in the morning of the 12th, Captain CURTIS sailed in the *Latona*, to apprize Lord HOWE of the situation of the Enemy's Fleet. At noon of that day, the British Squadron appeared in good order, off Estepona, or Marbella, and the Transports, with the Frigates, were working to windward, to gain the Bay. As they approached the Isthmus, the Enemy saluted them from their Mortars, and fired upon them from behind the Eastern Advanced Guard House.

The Combined Fleets, meanwhile, were very active in repairing their damages, and in forming a Line of Battle along the shore. In the evening of the 12th, a number of Troops were embarked on board them from the Camp. At night the *Panther* Man of War, with several of the British Transports, reached the Bay. The Enemy persevered in their Cannonade from their Land Batteries, and made some fruitless attempts with shells to burn the St. Michael. The fire from the Garrison was more than commonly brisk, as such a material supply of ammunition had been thrown in, and the effects were very perceptible in the Enemy's Works.

The spirits of the Garrison were uncommonly elevated by the flattering communications transmitted from home, in which their gallant and laborious services were stated to have received the particular approbation of their SOVEREIGN. In the Garrison Orders of the 12th, the following Extracts were inserted :

Extract

G. O. " Extract from a Letter to the Governor, from the Earl
" of SHELBURNE, one of HIS MAJESTY's Principal Se-
" cretaries of State.

Dated St. James's, July 10, 1782.

" I am also honoured with HIS MAJESTY's Command
" to assure you in the strongest terms, that no encourage-
" ment shall be wanting to the brave Officers and Soldiers
" under your command. His Royal Approbation of the
" past, will no doubt be a powerful incentive to future.
" exertions; and I have the KING's Authority to assure
" you, that every distinguished act of emulation and
" gallantry which shall be performed in the course of the
" Siege, by any, even of the lowest rank, will meet with
" ample reward from his gracious protection and favour.
" These HIS MAJESTY's intentions you will communicate
" to every part of your Garrison, that they may be perfectly
" satisfied, their Royal Master feels for the difficulties they
" are under, admires their glorious resistance, and will be
" happy to reward their merit."

" Extract from a Letter to the Governor, from the Right
" Honourable General CONWAY, Commander in Chief of
" HIS MAJESTY's Forces.

Dated August 31st, 1782.

" I am now to add, that I have the KING's Command to
" inform you, that he is in the greatest degree satisfied with
" the brave and steady defence made by your Garrison;
" and HIS MAJESTY is desirous of shewing them every
" mark of his Royal Approbation. It is in this light that
" HIS MAJESTY has been graciously pleased to consent to
" granting Bât and Forage Money, as a proper indulgence
" to your Officers."

Such marks of gracious attention on the part of their
Sovereign, could not fail to be highly gratifying to the
minds

minds of Soldiers—of men too, who felt they had achieved every thing that human valour, perseverance, and conduct could effect in the most perilous circumstances. They were now made sensible, that the highest reward attended them to which Military Ambition can aspire. They were possessed of the gracious favour of their Prince, and the grateful approbation of their Country. The Sentiments which such a consciousness naturally inspired, tended to render the united efforts of France and Spain still more abortive than they had even hitherto been, though the treasures and strength of one Nation had been exhausted in the conflict, and the military pride of the other had received a mortal wound.

On the 13th of October, the Combined Fleets weighed anchor, and stood out evidently with an intention of preventing the Transports from reaching the Garrison. They amounted to Forty-four Ships of the Line, with a vast number of Frigates and other smaller Vessels. By the superior conduct of the British Admiral, however, he was enabled to throw all the Supplies into the Garrison, and manœuvred his Fleet so as not to shun an Engagement, even with so marked a superiority of force as the Enemy opposed to him. He lay in a close line to leeward of the Combined Fleets, but they did not think it proper to profit by the advantage of the wind.

On the 18th, the *Buffalo* Man of War, with the rest of the Transports, got in, and at noon of the same day, four or five Ships of the Line, under the orders of Lord MULGRAVE, were detached to the Garrison with the 25th and 59th Regiments. His Lordship disembarked the Troops with the greatest expedition, and rejoined the Admiral

Admiral off Tetuan, who having now accomplished the object of his expedition, resolved to embrace the favourable wind that then prevailed, to carry him out to the Westward. On the following morning, therefore, at day break, Lord Howe, under an easy sail, stood with his Fleet in close order towards the Straits, the Combined Fleet, that was to the Eastward, and consequently to windward of him, steering the same course. On the preceding evening, Captain Curtis had gone off in the *Latona*, to communicate to the Admiral the Governor's confidential dispatches, and no opportunity offering for his return to the Garrison, he was obliged to remain on board the Fleet.

On the morning of the 20th, the wind shifted to the Northward, and Lord Howe having got clear of the Straits, he formed his Fleet to leeward, to receive the Enemy, who still kept the weather-gage. By this circumstance they were left, uninterruptedly, to take the distance at which they should think proper to engage; but in place of confiding in their great superiority, (for they had no less than 46 ships in their line) and aiming at a close and decisive Action, they began their Cannonade at sun-set on the Van and Rear of the British Fleet, seeming to point their chief attack on the latter, and continued their fire along their whole Line, at a considerable distance, and with little effect, until Ten at Night. The fire was only returned occasionally from different ships of the English Fleet, as the nearer approach of the Enemy at times afforded a more favourable opportunity for making any impression upon them.

As it was not the policy of the British Admiral to seek, with so very inferior a force, a renewal of the Action,

R   (particularly

(particularly as he had so successfully relieved the Garrison) and as the Enemy seemed studiously to shun a closer
Engagement, the Fleets separated in the night, the Combined Fleets having hauled their wind, and stood on with
a great press of sail.

The Garrison of Gibraltar, though they felt much
anxiety for the event of the Action, which would be particularly momentous to them, yet had the strongest reliance
upon the superior conduct and courage of British Officers
and Seamen. They were not, meanwhile, inattentive to
the operations of the Enemy on the Land side, who attempted to make some little additions to their Works,
notwithstanding a very brisk fire was constantly directed
upon them from the Garrison.

Towards the end of the Month, the Enemy had wholly
ceased working in their Approaches, and began to break
up their Camp. Every hope of subduing the Fortress
seemed to have been entirely relinquished. They still
continued their Cannonade, however, from their Works,
and their Gun-boats occasionally presented themselves
before the Walls; but these were generally soon obliged
to retire, and the former gradually diminished.

In the beginning of December the Enemy began to construct a mine in a Cave near the Devil's Tower, by which
they purposed to blow up the Northern part of the Rock.
On the absurdity of such a project, it is unnecessary to
enlarge, for what must be the nature of that mine that
could affect a solid rock of nearly fifteen hundred feet of
perpendicular height?

The

The Enemy, however, had been at work some time before they were discovered by the Garrison, who received the first intimation of their design, indeed, from a Deserter from the Walloon Guards. It appeared so extraordinary, that it did not at first find credence in the Garrison ; but numerous bodies of men being perceived approaching to the spot described, along the eastern shore, the circumstance attracted something more of the attention of the Governor. A lodgement was at length found, from whence a part of their Work could be overlooked, and they were from that period very sorely annoyed in its prosecution, as the Corps of Corsican Riflemen were posted on the lodgement, who did execution upon the Enemy whenever they appeared by day, and by night Cohorns were continually played off upon the spot.

From this period the Garrison was regularly visited by the Gun and Mortar Boats of the Enemy, which had been increased to the number of thirty or upwards. They sometimes did a considerable deal of damage, but at any rate very much harrassed the Troops. These Attacks were likewise seconded by a warm discharge from the Lines and Advanced Works. The Enemy seldom retired, however, without having suffered ; for in addition to the Batteries, Sir CHARLES KNOWLES, who now commanded the Gunboats belonging to the Garrison, always co-operated with spirit and success.

Such, after the defeat of their mighty projects in the month of September, 1782, was the petty warfare which the Spaniards carried on, till the 2d of February, 1783, when the Duc de CRILLON informed the Governor, by a Flag of Truce, that the Preliminaries of a General Peace

R 2   had

had been signed at Paris on the 20th of January, between Great Britain, France, and Spain. When the Boats met, the Spaniards rose up, in a seeming transport of joy, and cried out, " *We are all Friends!*"—delivering the Letters with the greatest apparent satisfaction. Previous to the meeting of the Boats, the Enemy discharged about thirty rounds, but never after the delivery of the Letters fired upon the Garrison. In the evening the British Artillery likewise ceased. On the following day, the Spaniards advanced from their Works, and conversed with the English Sentries; but this was an intercourse which the Governor prudently discouraged, till he should receive Official Confirmation from England of the Duc de CRILLON's Communications.

On the 5th of February the Duke informed the Governor, that the *Blockade* by sea was discontinued; in consequence of which a Placart was published in the Garrison, that the Port was again open.

It was not till the 10th of March that General ELIOTT received by the *Thetis* Frigate, Official Accounts from England, of the General Pacification which had taken place. These were conveyed by Sir ROGER CURTIS, who, upon his return to England with Lord HOWE, had been honoured with Knighthood for his gallant conduct on the 14th of September preceding, and who had otherwise received very flattering marks of HIS MAJESTY's Approbation.

On the evening of the 10th, the Duc de CRILLON sent a Parley to the Garrison, which was answered the succeeding day. The subject of this Correspondence was

to

to appoint an interview between the Generals; and on
the 12th the Duke, attended by his Suite, appeared at the
extremity of the Western Boyau, and immediately sent
an Aid-du-Camp to inform General Eliott he was
arrived. The latter, attended by Lieutenant Koehler,
one of his Aides-du-Camp, soon afterwards rode out by
Lower Forbes's, and was met by the Duke on the Beach,
half-way between the Works and Bay-Side Barrier..
Both at the same instant dismounted, and embraced.
They afterwards conversed for about half an hour, and
then returned to their respective posts. Hostilities at an
end, those great Generals could indulge in that intercourse
of mutual esteem, which their Military Conduct had re-
spectively impressed them with; and indeed the general
sentiment that pervaded both the British Garrison and
the Spanish Camp, seemed now to flow from the most
liberal philanthropy. Emulation in danger, and feats of
Arms, yielded to that generous social feeling which the
recollection of past danger, and relief from excessive hardship naturally inspires; and in proportion to the national
enmity which each had felt, seemed to be the degree
of esteem which they now reciprocally acknowledged.

The Spaniards were busily employed in dismantling
their Works, whilst the Garrison were repairing the
different Lines and Batteries that had sustained any damage.

On the 18th the Duke sent the Governor a Present of a
grey Andalusian Horse; and on the 23d the latter, accompanied by General Green, the Chief Engineer, and
their Aides-du-Camp, met the Duke in the Spanish
Works. They were conducted by him through the
whole,

whole, and afterwards to the Cave at the Devil's Tower. They dined on that day with the Duke at San Roque, and returned to the Garrison in the evening.

On the 31st the Duc de CRILLON, accompanied by the Marquis de SAYA, Prince de MESSARANO, Counts de JAMAÏQUE and de SERANO, the Intendant, and Captain TENDON, returned the Governor's visit. The Governor received the Duke and his Suite near Forbes's ; and on his entering the Garrison, a Salute was fired of seventeen pieces of Cannon from the Grand Battery. When the Duke appeared within the Walls, the Soldiers saluted him with a general Huzza! which being unexpected, it was said, greatly confused him. The circumstance, however, being explained to him, he seemed highly pleased with the old English custom ; and as he passed up the main street, where the ruinous and desolated appearance of the Town attracted a good deal of his observation, his Excellency behaved with great affability. ·

The Officers of the Garrison were introduced by Corps to the Duke, at the Convent. When those of the Artillery were presented, he received them with the most flattering distinction—" Gentlemen," said he, addressing himself to them, " I would rather see you here as Friends, " than on your Batteries as Enemies, where," added he, " you never spared me." His Excellency was afterwards conducted to the Batteries on the Heights. At *Willis's* he made some remarks on the formidable appearance of the lower defences ; observing, whilst he pointed towards the Old Mole Battery, that, " had not his opinion been " over-ruled, he should have directed all his efforts against " that part of the Garrison." This led to a conversation

about

about the Floating Batteries, in which the Duke pleasantly disclaimed the project of them as his own. After a fantastical preamble, he said to General ELIOTT, " that the " Chance of War was uncertain—that he had gone into " the Scheme of the Attack from the Floating Batteries, " because the King wished it should be tried : besides," he added, " they furnished him with bad machines ; and " his complaisance to the King had induced him to sup- " press other schemes more certain, and from which he " flattered himself he would have gained his (General " ELIOTT's) esteem."

The very perfect state of the Batteries produced some compliments to the Chief Engineer, and when conducted into the Gallery above Farringdon's Battery, the Duke was astonished, particularly when he was informed of its extent, which was at that time between five and six hundred feet. Turning to his Suite, after exploring the extremity, " These Works," he exclaimed, " are worthy of " the Romans."

At Dinner were present the Generals and Brigadiers of the Garrison, with their Suites. Amongst other things, i the course of the conversation, the Duke asked the General what he thought of the Mine that he had contrived at the foot of the Escarpments of the Rock ? The General was about to give an answer ; but the Duke, perceiving his idea by the smile on his countenance, prevented him, by saying, " Is it not true, General, that that Mine was a " farce ? But in War, as in every thing else, we must have " amusement, and on that account it was I ordered that " Gallery to be made, merely to amuse my Soldiers." The Duke, in the course of conversation, paid many Compliments to the Governor and Garrison, for their noble defence.

defence. "He had exerted himself," he said, "to the "utmost of his abilities; and though he had not been "successful, yet he was happy in having his Sovereign's "approbation of his conduct."

After dinner the Duke passed through the Camp to Europa, each Regiment turning out without Arms, and giving him three cheers as he passed. Having satisfied his curiosity, he returned by the way of Land-Port, to which he was conducted by the Governor, and upon his passing the Barrier of which, he was saluted with seventeen guns.

On the 2d of April, the Duke quitted the Camp, and took the route for Madrid. He was succeeded in command by Lieutenant-General the Marquis de SAYA.

HIS MAJESTY, as a mark of his Royal Approbation for the Defence of Gibraltar, having been pleased to confer upon General ELIOTT the Most Honourable Order of the Bath; and having signified his Royal Pleasure by Sir Roger CURTIS, that Lieutenant-General BOYD should act as HIS MAJESTY's Representative in investing the Governor with the Insignia of the Order; and further having expressed his desire that the same should be done with all the splendor and magnificence which the state of the Garrison would admit of, due preparations were made by the Engineers, which were not completed till the 23d of April. A grand Colonade was erected upon the King's Bastion, the post which General ELIOTT occupied during the signal VICTORY which he had obtained over the Combined Powers of France and Spain. At eight o'clock of the morning of that day, Detachments from all the Regiments and

and Corps, with all the Officers not on duty, were assembled in three lines on the Red-Sands. The Governor having taken post in the centre of the second line, after the usual Compliments had been paid, addressed the Garrison in the following words:

" GENTLEMEN,

" I have assembled you this day, in order that the
" Officers and Soldiers may receive, in the most public
" manner, an authentic Declaration transmitted to me
" by the Secretary of State, expressing the high sense
" HIS MAJESTY entertains of your meritorious conduct
" in Defence of this Garrison. The King's Satisfac-
" tion upon this event was soon divulged to all the World,
" by His most gracious Speech to both Houses of Par-
" liament, * The House of Lords and House of Com-
" mons not only made the suitable professions in their
" Addresses to the Throne, but have severally enjoined
" me to communicate their Unanimous Thanks by the
" following Resolutions:

" *Die Veneris*, 13 *Decembris*, 1782.

" Resolved, *nem. dis.*, by the Lords Spiritual and Tempo-
" ral, in Parliament assembled, that this House doth
" highly approve, and acknowledge the Services of the

S   " Officers,

----

* HIS MAJESTY, in His Speech from the Throne, December
5th, 1782, spoke with pride and satisfaction, of the gallant Defence
made by the Governor and Garrison of Gibraltar ; and of the honour
acquired by His Fleet, which had offered Battle to the Combined
Force of France and Spain upon their own Coasts.

" Officers, Soldiers, and Sailors, lately employed in
" the Defence of Gibraltar ; and that General ELIOTT
" do signify the same to them."

" *Die Jovis,* 12 *Decembris,* 1782.

" Resolved, *nem. con.,* That the Thanks of this House (of
" Commons) be given to Lieutenant-General BOYD,
" Major - General De la MOTTE, Major - General
" GREEN, Chief Engineer, to Sir ROGER CURTIS,
" Knight, and to the Officers, Soldiers, and Sailors,
" lately employed in the Defence of Gibraltar."

The Governor then proceeded.—" No Army has ever
" been rewarded by higher National Honours ; and it is
" well known, how great, universal, and spontaneous
" were the rejoicings throughout the Kingdom, upon the
" news of your Success. These must not only give you
" pleasure, but afford matter of triumph to your dearest
" friends and latest posterity. As a farther proof how
" just your title is to such flattering distinctions at home,
" rest assured, from undoubted authority, that the Na-
" tions in Europe, and other parts, are struck with ad-
" miration of your gallant behaviour : even our late re-
" solute and determined Antagonists do not scruple to be-
" stow the commendations due to such valour and perse-
" verance.

" I now must warmly congratulate you on these united
" and brilliant testimonies of Approbation, amidst such
" numerous, such exalted tokens of applause; and
" FORGIVE ME, FAITHFUL COMPANIONS, IF I HUMBLY
" CRAVE YOUR ACCEPTANCE OF MY GRATEFUL Ac-
" KNOWLEDGMENTS. I ONLY PRESUME TO ASK THIS
" FAVOUR,

" FAVOUR, AS HAVING BEEN A CONSTANT WITNESS OF
" YOUR CHEARFUL SUBMISSION TO THE GREATEST
" HARDSHIPS, YOUR MATCHLESS SPIRIT AND EXERTI-
" ONS, AND ON ALL OCCASIONS, YOUR HEROIC CON-
" TEMPT OF EVERY DANGER."

A grand *Feu-de-joie* was then fired by the Line, each
discharge commencing with a Royal Salute of twenty-one
guns. Three Cheers closed the ceremony.

On the same forenoon the Governor was invested with
the Order of the Bath, in the Colonade erected upon the
King's Bastion. The Ceremony was conducted with
the utmost pomp and magnificence. All the Soldiers of
the Garrison were regaled by the Governor, and the
whole concluded with a grand display of Fire-works in
the evening.

Thus gloriously closed the labours and dangers of the
Garrison of Gibraltar, who, during a period of *three years,
seven months, and twelve days,* had experienced every
hardship and fatigue incident to a state of the most active
warfare. Their courage, perseverance, and exertion, were
perhaps never equalled, certainly never surpassed. Their
uniform contempt of unremitting danger during so long
a period, justly entitles them to the admiration which
Heroism ever claims; while their strict regard to Discipline, and the arduous duties of their several stations, was
highly honourable to them both as Soldiers and as Men.
Instances of Heroic Spirit were frequently displayed,
which the liberal Historian would delight to dwell upon
with his warmest applause; but to particularize these,
would swell this Work far beyond the size of a common

Volume.

Volume. Each Corps, as it equally participated in the
perils and glories of the Siege, is entitled to its equal
portion of Military Fame; but none surely will deem it
a partial and invidious selection, if the ROYAL ARTIL-
LERY are deemed deserving of a more signal renown.
Their duty led them to be constantly in the Batteries,
and where every thing was effected by the Ordnance,
their services may be supposed to have been more than
generally eminent. Such was the impression which the
Duc de CRILLON, and the Combined Armies had received of them—such is the just tribute to their Military
Science and gallant Conduct, which not only the present
age, but all posterity must pay.

It were, perhaps, an injustice to the generosity of the
British Nation, to omit mentioning the marks of gratitude and applause which were universally bestowed upon
the Corps who had served at Gibraltar during the Siege,
upon their return to England. No Soldiers were ever
more honoured by their Countrymen, and none surely
ever deserved such honour more.

His MAJESTY, as a testimony of his Approbation towards the Hanoverian Corps employed at Gibraltar, ordered a Scarf to be presented to every Soldier, to be
worn on the arm, having on it a Motto descriptive of the
glorious service for which it was bestowed. His MA-
JESTY further ordered, that all the Men who had been
engaged in the service of the Garrison, belonging to those
Corps, should receive, when they became Pensioners,
double the allowance given to ordinary Soldiers. The
Grenadiers of these Corps were likewise ordered to bear
upon their Caps a Silver Plate, given by His MAJESTY,

with

with the word GIBRALTAR inscribed upon it in distinguished characters.

Nothing, in short, was left unperformed, which the Justice and Munificence of the Sovereign, and the Gratitude of the Nation could bestow. The Troops engaged in the Defence of Gibraltar, however, may confidently look for a still further reward: the record of their services will fill an honourable page in the Military Annals, not only of their own Country, but of Europe ;—and while the Character of the British Nation is raised and honoured by their gallantry, mankind, through every age, will unite in honouring them.

THE END.

ABSTRACT OF THE LOSS OF THE GARRISON DURING THE SIEGE.

	O.	S.	D.	R.&F.
Killed, and dead of wounds	6	25	4	298
Disabled by wounds (discharged)	3	13	2	120
Dead of Sickness, exclusive of those who died of the Scurvy in 1779, and 1780 }	7	22	2	505
Discharged from incurable Complaints	0	00	0	181
Deserted	0	00	0	43
	16	60	8	1147

EXPENDITURE OF AMMUNITION
FROM THE

GARRISON.		ENEMY.	
Rounds	200,600	Rounds, all heavy ...	244,104
British Gun-boats, shot	4,788	Spanish Gun-boats, shot and shells }	14,283
	205,388		258,387

The Garrison expended very near 8000 barrels of powder; and the number of Ordnance damaged and destroyed during the Siege, amounted to 53.

The number of barrels of powder expended by the Enemy could never be ascertained, nor what Ordnance were destroyed.

POSTSCRIPT.

Mr. Poggi cannot permit his Print of the *Sortie* made by the GARRISON of GIBRALTAR, to go into the World, without making those Acknowledgments to Individuals, which Justice and Gratitude equally suggest. He feels it a particular duty to express his obligations to the late Lieut. Col. HARDY, formerly Quarter-Master General of the Garrison—to Sir JAMES FOULIS, Town-Major and Aid-du-Camp, and to Major VALLOTTON, First Aid-du-Camp to General ELIOTT. He has likewise particular obligations to Captain BOOTH, of the Corps of Engineers, who favoured him with the Drawings which he had made in progression, of the Spanish Advanced Batteries and Camps, as the former were erected previous to, and completed at the time of the *Sortie*. From the Drawings likewise of Captain HISLOP of the 39th Regiment, and Lieut. SANBY of the 12th, and of Lieut. MACKERRAS of the Engineers, he gained very important knowledge of the Subjects upon which he occupied his Pencil during his residence at Gibraltar. He was also much assisted in ascertaining the exact position of the Detachment, and the distribution of the different Working Parties, by seeing an excellent Drawing made by Lieutenant KOEHLER of the Royal Artillery, and Aid-du-Camp to the General, and with which General ELIOTT furnished Mr. POGGI for the purpose. From several other Officers of the Garrison of Gibraltar, while he was there, Mr. POGGI experienced

perienced very great attention, and assistance in the execution of his Work, of which favours he retains a very
grateful remembrance.

Mr. Poggi trusts he will be excused, if he makes, in
this place, respectful mention of the Labours of the
Artist by whom his Plate has been engraved. Mr.
Pouncey's industry must be allowed to be equal to the
professional ability which he has displayed in this work,
when it is known that it has been the constant labour of
upwards of Seven Years. The accuracy and delicacy of
the finishing in a piece so minute in its parts, and so uncommonly large in its dimensions, are not less conspi-
cuous than the admirable effect produced by the harmony
of the colours, which so faithfully represents a Night
Scene, illuminated only by the flames, the explosion of a
Mortar, and the fire from the Spanish Lines. Mr.
Poggi feels a solicitude that every degree of justice should
be done to Merit, which in that professional line, he
presumes to think has seldom been surpassed.

DESCRIPTION

OF

MR. POGGI's PRINT

OF THE

Sortie made by the Garrison of Gibraltar,

On the Morning of the 27th of November, 1781.

THE front ground represents part of the Gardens that formerly belonged to the Garrison, in which is Lieutenant Cuppage of the Royal Artillery, in the act of commending the two Artillery Soldiers, Campbell and Paton, for their humanity to Baron Helmstadt; and directing them to convey him to the Garrison, in which humane and generous office he himself assisted. Several wounded British Soldiers are seen lying on the ground in the Gardens, and others are in the act of being conducted to that spot.

The *Reserve*, consisting of the Grenadier and Light Companies of the 56th and 58th Regiments, under Major Maxwell of the 73d Regiment, (who appears in the interval between the two Grenadier Companies, in his Highland dress) occupies the front.

A little to the right of the Light Company forming the left of the Reserve, is Lieutenant Tweedie, of the 12th Regiment, conveyed by three Grenadiers into the Garrison.

T   Beyond

Beyond these is the 12th Regiment, drawn up in front of the Batteries, the drums in the rear; and a little to the left of them, a party of Spanish Prisoners on their way to the Garrison.

In the front of the St. Carlos Battery is posted General ELIOTT, attending to Sir JAMES FOULIS, who is in the act of pointing to the Hanoverian Ordonnance dispatched by Colonel HUGO. Behind General ELIOTT are Lieut. Colonel HARDY, Quarter-Master-General, Major VAL-LOTTON, First Aid-du-Camp, and Lieutenant KOEHLER of the Royal Artillery, Aid-du-Camp to the General. Behind them are three Orderly Serjeants. At the feet of Sir JAMES FOULIS lies Don JOSEPH BARBOZA, Captain of the Spanish Artillery, who was mortally wounded at the first onset of the British Troops.

Near the Colours of the 12th Regiment are represented Brigadier-General Ross, and Lieutenant-Colonel DA-CHENHAUSEN; the latter in the act of pointing out to the former the person of General ELIOTT. The Brigadier in an attitude of surprize.

A little to the right of the 12th Regiment is a small party of Spanish Prisoners, under the conduct of two British Grenadiers. Further to the right is HARDEN-BERG's Regiment of Hanoverians, drawn up in front of the East Parallel. Beyond the right extremity of the same Parallel are the Grenadiers of REDEN's and LA MOTTE's, Lieutenant-Colonel HUGO appearing to the front between the intervals.

On the top of the St. Carlos Battery is the Highlander who encountered with Don JOSEPH BARBOZA, and who having

having mortally wounded him, was himself wounded by
that Officer. The centre of the flame from that Battery
expresses the explosion which took place in spiking one of
the Mortars, occasioned by the friction of the grain, which
caused the Mortar, that was loaded, to explode.

All along the Batteries, the Workmen of the British
Detachment are in the act of demolishing the Works,
and preparing them for the fire-faggots.—On the top of
the Six Gun Battery furthest to the left, is Captain CUR-
TIS, who went out as a Volunteer with General ELIOTT, in
the act of brandishing his Sword, and calling to the Sailors
to come on, who are running in a group beneath him,
with pick-axes and fire-faggots on their shoulders, and
waving their hats in triumph.

Immediately behind the front parapet of the St. Carlos
Battery is represented Captain WITHAM of the Royal
Artillery, in the act of seizing Don VINCENTE FRIZA,
the Spanish Lieutenant of Artillery, by the sword hand, the
former having only a match stock in his hand.

Within the Mill Battery are posted the 39th, and close
along the fourth Branch of Approach the 73d Flank Companies. The 72d Flank Companies with their right to the
extremity of the fourth Branch, and their left to the Beach.

In the centre of the St. Carlos Battery is the old Mill
Tower.

To the left of the St. Carlos, is the St. Paschal Mortar
Battery, and a little behind it, inclining towards the Beach
of Gibraltar-Bay, are the two Six Gun Batteries.

In

In the front of Reden's and La Motte's Grenadiers, is the Centre Stone Guard-House, before which the Spanish Troop of Horse passed, and challenged the Hanoverians. They afterwards, as represented, galloped off towards the Centre Barrier of their Lines, but were obliged, in consequence of the brisk fire from the Garrison upon that spot, to wheel off to the right towards Fort St. Barbara. Parties of the Spaniards are represented flying towards their Lines in different directions.

On the right is Fort St. Barbara firing upon the Garrison. To the left of it is a Mortar Battery, in one of the *Place d'Armes*, from which the Enemy are throwing a shell. From the Battery La Princessa, in the centre of the Lines, is represented an horizontal fire upon the Garrison. To the right of the Lines is Fort St. Philip, which is silent. A little further to the left is La Batteria del Rey, or the Black Battery, above which is the Town of San Roque—a little to the left of that is Buena Vista, and a little to the rear, between Fort St. Philip and the Black Battery, is the Spanish Camp. Behind the Battery communicating with the first Line of Approach, is the mountain known by the name of the Queen of Spain's Chair, upon the top of which is a repeating Signal House. The whole is bounded by the distant Mountains of the Provinces of Andalusia on the left, and Grenada on the right.

To the right of Fort St. Barbara is part of the Mediterranean Sea—to the left of Fort St. Philip, part of the Bay of Gibraltar. ✓